Praise for *Getting Grief Right*

"With profound compassion and juicy storytelling, Patrick O'Malley offers those of us whose lives have been shattered by loss permission to mourn our loved ones with all our hearts and find our own transformational stories in the crucible of our authentic life experiences."

MIRABAI STARR
author of *Caravan of No Despair: A Memoir of Loss and Transformation*; translator of *Dark Night of the Soul (St. John of the Cross)*

"*Getting Grief Right* is a compassionate, wise, and practical guide that gives space for our grief to tell its own story and be as it is. A very valuable, up-to-date resource for anyone wanting to consciously navigate this challenging inner landscape."

JOHN J. PRENDERGAST, PHD
author of *In Touch: How to Tune In to the Inner Guidance of Your Body and Trust Yourself*; psychotherapist; adjunct professor of psychology (retired), California Institute of Integral Studies

"Avoiding clichés and shattering the idea that grief marches through some predictable and lock-step set of 'stages,' O'Malley instead understands that every experience of grief is personal and unique and that every griever has a story worth telling. This book is immensely valuable, both for those who grieve and for those who want to offer them true consolation."

THOMAS G. LONG
coauthor of *The Good Funeral: Death, Grief, and the Community of Care*

"*Getting Grief Right* offers both individual mourners and grief groups a restorative approach to handling grief, while preserving memories of our loved ones. O'Malley and Madigan . . . offer a template for the reader's grief journey that works in both private and group settings. I highly recommend the book's study guide for anyone interested in honoring their own grief journey or eager to help others who have recently experienced loss."

CANDI CANN, PHD
associate professor of religion at Baylor University and author of
Virtual Afterlives: Grieving the Dead in the Twenty-First Century

"Patrick O'Malley touches an issue dear to my heart and mind: the importance of telling the truth about loss, which is really the truth about love . . . He normalizes grief, offering it back to the griever to explore and define their own experience within the wide frame of health and wellness."

MEGAN DEVINE
teacher, speaker, psychotherapist, and author of *It's OK That You're Not OK: Meeting Grief and Loss in a Culture That Doesn't Understand*

"O'Malley validates my experience of ministering for forty-five years to grieving people: they want to, they need to, talk about and remember their loved ones who died. He helps us understand what is unique about each person's grief story, and how our grief story is our 'therapy.'"

FR. CHARLES CALABRESE
chaplain, Texas Health Harris Methodist Hospital Fort Worth

"Patrick O'Malley has created a subtle, honest, and delicate understanding of living a life of grief. *Getting Grief Right* is not a list of stages or rules; it does not pretend to know about the grief of others. Because O'Malley, a psychotherapist, himself suffered the inconsolable loss of the death of his child, he can accompany others through their grieving. His book becomes a warm, accepting presence, telling stories and inviting readers to tell their own. Grieving does not end, O'Malley softly notes, but the stories that we tell about those we have lost turn the grief right back into the love from which it springs."

RITA CHARON, MD, PHD
professor of medicine at Columbia University Medical Center;
executive director, Program in Narrative Medicine

"A must-read for anyone who is grieving the loss of a loved one. When it comes to professionals, Dr. Patrick O'Malley is the best of the best. This book is a special gift to the world and sure to become a classic."

KEN DRUCK, PHD
author of *The Real Rules of Life: Balancing Life's Terms with Your Own*

"Dr. Patrick O'Malley is a very wise, compassionate storyteller . . . He helps us understand that to mourn and grieve is as natural as breathing. We ask, 'How long will it take?' Dr. O'Malley says, 'How deeply did you love?' This book is a masterpiece that will touch your heart and soul with healing powers."

PEGGY BOHME
cofounder of The WARM Place Grief Support Center
for Children in Fort Worth, Texas

GETTING
GRIEF
RIGHT

Also by Tim Madigan

*See No Evil: Blind Devotion and Bloodshed
in David Koresh's Holy War*

*The Burning: Massacre, Destruction,
and the Tulsa Race Riot of 1921*

I'm Proud of You: My Friendship with Fred Rogers

Every Common Sight: A Novel

PATRICK O'MALLEY, PHD
with TIM MADIGAN

GETTING
GRIEF
RIGHT

FINDING YOUR STORY of LOVE
in the SORROW
of LOSS

sounds true
BOULDER, COLORADO

Sounds True
Boulder, CO 80306

This book is not intended as a substitute for the medical recommendations of physicians, mental health professionals, or other healthcare providers. Rather, it is intended to offer information to help the reader cooperate with physicians, mental health professionals, and health providers in a mutual request for optimum well-being. We advise readers to carefully review and understand the ideas presented and to seek the advice of a qualified professional before attempting to use them.

All client stories offered in this book are composites. No story reflects any specific individual, and all circumstances and names have been changed to protect identities.

Published 2017

Cover design by Jennifer Miles
Book design by Beth Skelley

Printed in Canada

Library of Congress Cataloging-in-Publication Data
Names: O'Malley, Patrick, author. | Madigan, Tim.
Title: Getting grief right : finding your story of love in the sorrow of loss
    / Patrick O'Malley, PhD with Tim Madigan.
Description: Boulder, CO : Sounds True, Inc., [2017] |
    Includes bibliographical references.
Identifiers: LCCN 2016049777 (print) | LCCN 2017012792 (ebook) |
    ISBN 9781622038206 (ebook) | ISBN 9781622038190 (pbk.)
Subjects: LCSH: Grief. | Loss (Psychology)
Classification: LCC BF575.G7 (ebook) | LCC BF575.G7 .O53 2017
    (print) | DDC 155.9/37—dc23
LC record available at https://lccn.loc.gov/2016049777

10 9 8 7 6 5 4 3 2

For Nancy, my beloved partner for life.
And in memory of our son, Ryan Palmer O'Malley.

For Catherine from Tim: I am because we are.

CONTENTS

Introduction

WHAT'S WRONG WITH ME?

When Mary first sat down in my office, six months after losing her daughter to sudden infant death syndrome, she had already hired and fired two other therapists. The bereaved mother was clearly trying to get her grief right.

A successful businesswoman in her thirties, she was unaccustomed to the weight of sorrow; she was an "up" person who could cheerfully handle almost anything that came her way. Mary was proud of that persona and worked hard to maintain it, even in the face of such a wrenching tragedy. Within a few days of her daughter's death, Mary was back at work, seeming to function largely as before. She was gracious when coworkers offered condolences but quickly insisted on turning conversations back to the task at hand. She said she was "doing fine." Indeed, she seemed to have "moved on," so convincing was the mask that she put on for the world each day.

The truth was another matter, as became increasingly undeniable to her and those around her. The effort to maintain the positive veneer sapped more and more of her energy. She started making uncharacteristic mistakes at work and found herself being short and overly critical with her employees.

"I really need to get back to my old self," she told me the day in the late 1990s when we met. "You would think I would be at least a little closer to that by now. I'm totally exhausted. I don't know how much longer I can keep this up. I hope you can help me."

Mary was by then fully acquainted with the five stages of grief—that famous gospel of mourning based on psychiatrist Elisabeth Kübler-Ross's 1969 book, *On Death and Dying*. Like the typical grieving person (then and now), Mary expected that the pain of loss would proceed through the stages of denial, anger, bargaining, depression, and finally, acceptance. The gospel also implied that an emotionally healthy person should grieve only so deeply and for only so long. For Mary, six months seemed like a reasonable amount of time.

But what if a person's mourning doesn't conform? When her sorrow lingered beyond the accepted norms, Mary felt that she had broken the rules somehow. That was why she and so many other clients had sought me out as a therapist—not only because of their heartbreak, but also because they felt they could not get their grief right.

In our first visit, Mary insisted that she was "stuck" in depression, which, in her mind, was keeping her from achieving acceptance and closure. Her questions were straight out of the Kübler-Ross theory: "Am I in denial? Am I angry enough?"

A few years earlier, I would have wondered those things myself and reviewed the stages, as Mary clearly had, looking for the stage where her "grief work" remained incomplete. I also would have zeroed in on her suspected depression. Was there a family history? Had she been depressed before? Were the antidepressants helping? Did she suffer from a chronic mental illness, or was her depression temporary and situational?

But by the time we met, I had begun to approach grief in a much different way. I was a grieving person myself, and I understood too well what Mary was going through. In the previous decade, I had traveled a dark road similar to hers: I had mourned the tragic loss of my own baby son. I had been a young therapist who had tried desperately to get my grief "right." I had felt stuck in my mourning and had asked myself many of the same questions that Mary asked herself. I could relate to the confusion and the nagging sense of inadequacy when my suffering did not conform to the orthodoxy. I knew the exhaustion of pretending. I knew the loneliness and isolation when the support of others began to fade while my pain did not.

It was in the course of that excruciating journey, and thanks largely to the unique privilege of spending thousands of hours with bereaved clients like Mary, that I came upon a new understanding of grief and grievers and learned the life-changing lessons that are the heart of this book. I began to understand why grief defied categorization, and I saw the fallacy of thinking that grief occurs in a predictable, linear way, one stage after another, until resolution is achieved.

I was steadily drawn to another way of understanding and even embracing the experience of mourning—through the narrative of grief. It might sound simplistic, but I discovered that our stories were indeed the pathway to living with loss.

"All sorrows can be borne if you put them in a story or tell a story about them," author Isak Dinesen once said.[1] This book is an invitation for you to do just that.

In the pages to come, I will help you both create and more deeply explore your story of grief. To help guide and inspire you, I will share my story and the stories I've heard from clients over the years. In fact, as you read, try imagining yourself in Mary's place, sitting across from me in my office. In that safe and nonjudgmental space, you will be free not only to tell the story of the one you lost but also to feel whatever previously stifled emotions might arise. You will unearth memories and feelings that you might not have come across otherwise. You will stop analyzing your grief and begin to honor your story of loss and to live it.

Indeed, I want to make clear at the outset that this book offers no promise that grief will end. I understand as well as anyone why we would wish that to be true. Mourning is painful. But it's unreasonable to think that parents who have lost a child or a person who has lost a loved one to suicide or a spouse who has lost a partner of fifty years won't grieve, to one extent or another, for the rest of their lives.

The writer Anne Lamott said it beautifully: "If you haven't already, you will lose someone you can't live without, and your heart will be badly broken, and you never completely get over the loss of a deeply beloved person. But this is also good news. The person lives forever, in your broken heart that doesn't seal back up. And you come through, and you learn to dance with the banged-up heart."[2]

This book and your own narrative of grief will help you learn to dance—that is, to move beyond the cruel but pervasive misconceptions into a larger truth. In the process of remembering, embracing, and sharing your own story, you will be liberated from the expectations of society and your own self-diagnosis and self-criticism about whether you are grieving correctly. This book will not help you "get over" your grief, but it will help you experience your sorrow in its purest form.

Your narrative of grief will help you more deeply understand your relationship to the one you lost and will, in turn, help you understand the pain you feel now.

Your narrative of grief might actually allow you to deepen your connection to the deceased.

This courageous exercise of feeling and remembering will help you become a more authentic, wise, and compassionate human being who will be better able to support others who mourn.

Getting Grief Right is written not only for those who grieve but also for those who seek to better support bereaved people in their lives but who do not yet have the knowledge to do so. To that end, I offer specific guidance that will allow you to go beyond the painful awkwardness and empty clichés and to be with a grieving person in ways that truly make a difference.

Few things could be more important than learning how to live with our sorrow and to support others who are bereaved. One thing is certain: grief is inevitable and inescapable. If we love, we will also grieve.

Chapter 1

A THERAPIST GRIEVES

As a young boy, I remember wondering things like, Why does everyone laugh at that kid? Why does my friend's dad never smile? Why is that boy so mean when that girl is always so nice? A basic curiosity about my fellow humans has always been a part of me. In high school I was also the person that friends (and occasionally teachers!) sought out to share their troubles with. My choice of careers thus seemed preordained.

I graduated with a psychology degree from the University of Texas and went on to earn a master's in counseling in 1979. My first job at a nonprofit counseling agency in my hometown was the realization of a professional dream.

Psychotherapy was new and cutting edge then, a time when the self-help movement was gathering steam and the stigma of therapy had lessened. New therapeutic interventions were proliferating. Psychodrama, family therapies, hypnosis—bold methods with cathartic outcomes—were exciting new options for clients suffering from anxiety, depression, or troubled relationships.

In those early days, I was particularly drawn to working with children and teens, which really meant working with their families. I would cram parents and siblings into my tiny office and try to help them understand how family dynamics might be contributing to a young person's suffering. I would gently cajole and provoke couples and children to try to get them to a healthier place. The work was extremely gratifying.

At home, I shared that exhilarating time with Nancy, my college sweetheart. We were married in 1974, and six years later, in the spring of 1980, learned that she was pregnant with our first child. That's when difficult realities began to intrude on our idyllic young lives.

Nancy, not due to deliver for three months, was awakened one night by a strange physical sensation. She wanted to get it checked out, just to be safe. The next morning—the day after Labor Day, to be exact—we found ourselves sitting in her obstetrician's office. After the examination, her doctor said we needed to get to the hospital. Labor had begun.

I remember how Nancy's voice trembled.

"Can a baby this premature live?" she asked.

"I don't know," the doctor said. "We will try to buy time. He will be a pipsqueak of a kid."

Thirty-six hours later, on September 3, 1980, Ryan Palmer O'Malley was born, weighing a little over two pounds. You couldn't have imagined a more fragile-looking creature. He had been far from ready to leave his mother's womb, yet there he was. In the first few moments of his life, I was aware of the great risk of loving my son, but I was powerless to resist doing so. From the first glimpse of Ryan, I knew he would have a place in my heart forever.

His early life was a succession of seemingly endless days and nights. We hovered over the side of his crib in the hospital, looking down at our boy who was hooked up to all this noisy equipment. His life was measured in minutes and hours. On several terrifying occasions, Ryan stopped breathing, and his medical team would rush in to resuscitate.

All that time, Nancy and I yearned to hold him, but his frailty and the equipment made it impossible. The most we could do was touch a tiny finger, rub a tiny arm. Instead of cooing, the sounds around my son were the mechanical beeping of intensive-care machines. Instead of that wonderful new baby smell, there was the pungent scent of the antiseptic soap we had to use to scrub up before seeing him. Despite not being able to hold him, despite all the machines between him and us, we loved him deeply.

Early fall turned to Thanksgiving and then to Christmas. Our son gradually grew stronger. One day in January, his doctor weaned him from the respirator. We could finally hold him without the tangle of tubes and wires.

On March 9, 1981, our seventh wedding anniversary, we were finally able to bring our baby home to hold him, bathe him, kiss him, dance with him, feed him, and rock him. He smiled for the first time in those days. Though he was still fragile and underweight, we allowed ourselves to start imagining Ryan's future. No parents loved a son more.

And then he was gone.

On Saturday night, May 16, 1981, we were treating him for a cold but were not particularly concerned; we had been through much worse. But early Sunday morning, our precious son suddenly stopped breathing. I started CPR. Ryan's doctor and an ambulance were at our house within minutes. His doctor administered a shot of adrenaline to his heart as the medical technicians continued CPR. Nancy and I silently prayed as we followed the speeding ambulance to the hospital.

The next several hours are a series of snapshots forever imprinted in my mind.

- His physician coming into the waiting room with tears in his eyes, saying, "I could not save him"

- Holding Ryan's body

- Returning home without him

- The heartbreak of our family and friends as we broke the news of his death

- The dreamlike, adrenaline-fueled rituals of visitation and funeral

- The faces of all those who filled the church

- The sight of his tiny casket by the altar

- Seeing construction workers removing their hard hats as the funeral procession drove by

- Leaving the cemetery on that sunny spring day

In the days after the funeral, Nancy and I disappeared into the mountains of New Mexico.

"We've been in a cabin in the mountains for three days," I wrote in my journal. "Normally a setting like this gives us boundless energy. [Now] we wait for the minutes to pass. We talk incessantly. We talk about him and about all the people involved in his life and in our life. We go over his last hours a hundred times out loud and God knows how many times to ourselves."

Although I was emotionally numb after Ryan died, I went back to work within a week. My bosses were supportive, and I could have taken more time, as I probably had no business seeing clients in that mental state. But I had no clue what I needed, what I was supposed to do. I was twenty-eight years old, and for all of my training, I had no experience with personal loss.

Some of my clients had heard about what had happened. I accepted their expressions of condolence but quickly tried to turn sessions back to their problems. I was trained to make sure I was taking care of them and not the other way around. But there were some awkward moments. I remember how some clients apologized for talking about their anxiety or unruly adolescents when my tragedy seemed so much worse.

I hope I did passable work, but frankly, I don't know if I did. I'm sure my attention span was terrible, and I often thought I should have taken another week before returning to my office and clients. Knowing what I know now, I realize at least a full month would have helped. In the weeks after Ryan died, I felt nothing but relief when a session was over and even more relief when the day was done and I no longer had to concentrate.

It was summer when my shock faded and the extent of my heartbreak became clear. I sought refuge in typical "escape" behaviors—"happy" hours and late nights, partying after work with my young colleagues. Yet I couldn't out-party my loss. One minute I would be jolly and engaging; the next, consumed by sorrow. I remember a couple of times disappearing into the bathroom at parties to weep. I would be out with the guys having a beer and would duck away when I felt the tears coming.

At home, sleepless nights followed one upon the next. I lay in bed, haunted by the memories—Ryan's first smile, followed by the moment he was driven off in the ambulance. And the questions—always the questions. What if he had lived? What would he be like now? What could we have done differently?

Recently, for the first time in probably twenty years, I reread my journal from that painful period. The words still caused my heart to sink and tears to well. As I reread those pages, I felt great compassion for Nancy and myself, the young couple who had to endure such a loss. We were younger than my two grown sons, Kevan and Connor, are now.

MAY 31, 1981

It has been two weeks. It seems like yesterday, and it seems like forever. Went to church today, and I couldn't look at the altar without imagining his casket being there. Work wasn't as bad as I expected. I cried several times Monday, which helped. I guess it is good to pretend to not be miserable. We've been out every night. It feels empty around here. Thursday was a very hard day for me. Thursday afternoons were usually "our" time together. So I walked in and went straight to his room and thought I would explode with missing him. I awakened early this morning thinking of two weeks ago. Going over every detail—those scenes are so clear. It's easier to picture him dead in some ways. It's so painful to remember him when he felt good and was smiling.

JUNE 6, 1981

One more sleepless night. Will Saturday nights and Sunday mornings be reminders of what I've lost forever? If not, then when will the Saturday and Sunday come that I don't spend most of the hours going over and over those final scenes? The distractions are waning, which means his death is slowly becoming more real. How could he have been smiling so three days before he died?

JUNE 23, 1981

Ten years ago I was writing thank-you notes to people who were celebrating my high school graduation. Tonight I write thank-yous to people who responded to my son's death. Growing up doesn't seem like a good deal tonight. The pain isn't much better. The emptiness is worse. The nights (and days) are longer. We bought a grave marker two weeks ago. Last week they put down a temporary one with his name on it. Not easy to see his name on the ground over a grave. His name belongs on his door, on his things, on his school papers and artwork.

AUGUST 17, 1981

Three months today. I think of him more often. My high school reunion and a friend's wedding have come and gone. People asking me how many children I have. One even [told] me how lucky I was I didn't have any because they are so much trouble. I had imagined the . . . "show off your kids" part of the reunion a hundred times, but I was empty-handed. Surely the proudest day of my life was when I took him to work and so many people saw him. I was so very proud.

NOVEMBER 17, 1981

Six months gone. It's been long since I've written. Not many ask about him lately. Some of those closest to me don't ask. I wish they would. Those who do, help a great deal. I believe the holidays will be sad without you. Being with other babies is still very sad. I moved my stuff into Ryan's room tonight. It still seems as though it is your room, although your things are packed away. The smell of your room lingers just a bit. This is my office now, but I'm filled with thoughts of you. Rocking you, changing you, watching you sleep. I've put my favorite picture of you and me out. I want to see it every day, although it hurts.

In another journal entry from just a week after Ryan's death, I wrote: "What 'stage' am I in? Still denying, I think. When will I get angry?"

Because of my training as a therapist, those were my expectations of mourning. If I was conscientious about my "grief work," faced up to the pain, didn't stuff my feelings, and "let go" of my son, then, I believed, I was destined to achieve emotional resolution. Grief felt like a toxic substance, something foreign that had invaded my body like a fever, something to be expelled. That feeling was consistent with linear models like the stages of grief. It was an illness to be cured, a wound to be healed.

And fight it I would. I would face up to my pain and thus be able get back to my life as before, without the cloud of sadness stalking me day after day. *Closure* was another word for it. One writer also called it the "psychological finish line."[1]

I spent the first anniversary of Ryan's death at his grave for a profoundly emotional several hours. It was unfathomable to me that his little body was in the ground just a few feet away. I imagined him beginning to walk and talk as a toddler of nearly two, of all the little milestones we would never experience.

I wrote in my journal that day:

> The magic year has passed. I am somewhat healed, although when given a few specific thoughts, I feel intense heartache. I walked through the cemetery today and was astonished at the ways people honor the dead. Our acknowledgment of Ryan is most simple. I looked at pictures and read old cards and letters. My memory is incredibly fresh when thinking about the Sunday to Sunday—the week of his death. The rest of the year is fuzzy.

> Many sleepless nights—that peculiar ringing in my ears when I talk about him for the first time to new acquaintances. Certainly I have thought of him on [each of the] . . . three hundred sixty-five days. I will continue to define our relationship.

I expected relief after that first anniversary, but the second year seemed just as painful. That year, having experienced very little relief from my sadness, I sought out one of my town's leading therapists. Based on his reputation, I was confident he could help me resolve my grief.

"I keep waiting for closure," I told him in our first session. "It's coming up on two years. I expected to be past this by now."

"It does seem that something is incomplete," he said. "You haven't let go of your son."

"It's not for lack of trying," I said.

"We have some work to do here," he said.

He gestured to an empty chair near us in his office.

"See Ryan there," he said. "Put your little boy in that chair."

I squirmed. I had done this exercise with clients and in training, but it was most uncomfortable having the tables turned. I did as I was told.

"Now tell him what he means to you," the therapist said. "Tell him how much you miss him. Tell him how much you love him."

I did, sobbing.

"Now tell Ryan this," he said. "You'll always love him, but you need to let him go."

More sobs.

"I'll always love you, Son, but I need to let you go."

I was grateful for those tears and the chance to speak my love and yearning for him. By then, I no longer felt comfortable talking about Ryan with friends, and they didn't ask about him either. It had been months since I had had a cleansing cry.

As I spoke to my son in the chair, the internalized emotion came pouring out. The therapist commended me. I had done everything that could be asked of a mourning person.

But that session did not provide the conversion experience I had hoped for. It did not resolve my sadness. Speaking with another in that safe environment, I could touch my sadness, feel it, but it didn't go away. I lived in a state of confusion. Either there was more work to be done, or I wasn't doing it the right way.

Nancy became pregnant again a year after Ryan's death, in the summer of 1982. We lived the next nine months with a knot in our stomachs, but our second son, Kevan, came into the world the picture of health. The anxiety didn't end there, though. Nancy and I were vigilant in the early months of his life, checking to make sure little Kevan was breathing. But we were also ecstatic, as were our parents, other relatives, and friends. No one was happier than my dad, Bill, who relished his new role as grandfather and occasional babysitter.

From the time I was young, I had sensed a shadow surrounding my father. As I grew older, I learned much more about the great suffering in his life. He had lost both of his parents and his only brother by the time he was twenty-five. He was also the typical Irishman—a mixture of tough and tender, bluster and kindness, a storyteller with a gregarious personality and a great sense of humor.

He was always my biggest fan. It seemed like he never missed a chance to tell me how proud he was of me. It pleased him so much that I was doing work that I loved. He had struggled to find his calling in life and wanted nothing more than for his children to find theirs.

When Nancy had gone into premature labor with Ryan, I brought her to the hospital, where doctors began attempts to delay delivery. I was beside myself. On my way home to pick up some things for the hospital stay, I stopped by the place where my dad worked.

"What's wrong, Boy?" he said.

I could barely get the words out, and he gave me a hug. Then Dad headed for the hospital to join the long vigil. Many months into Ryan's hospital stay, when we were able to hold and rock him, my dad relished his turns to cradle his tiny grandson. And no one was more joyful when we could finally bring Ryan home. Dad stayed with him one night so Nancy and I could get out for a few hours. When we returned, the size of Dad's grin betrayed his pride.

"We had a good chat," he said. "I gave him his bottle."

Dad also had a poet's heart. He did not often reveal it, but there was no concealing it after Ryan died. It was my father who gave me the blank journal to write my story. He wasn't a particularly psychologically sophisticated fellow, but he knew what I needed. He tucked the following note inside the journal:

> Think of Ryan as one of these large foundations that give gifts to worthy causes. Except that Ryan can give a gift of love. He received so much love from so many people in his short life that he can return it for you or anyone else who thinks of him. If you ever feel depressed, think of him (I know you will think of him always), and he will share that love with you so that you can go on to face life, and that life is better for having him with you if only for such a short time.

Nearly two years later, on Saturday, May 14, 1983, Dad came by our home in his old Mustang. He said he wanted me to help him try to figure out a minor mechanical problem. I think it was really his excuse to get to see Kevan, his new grandson, who had been born three months earlier. The next afternoon, I got a call that my dad had not shown up for work.

He had recently been treated for heart problems, but I tried not to think the worst as I raced to the apartment where he lived alone. He was sitting in a chair, his body visible through the window, but the door was locked. He wouldn't answer. I tried to convince myself that he was just in a particularly deep sleep. The apartment manager let me in. Dad had one leg comfortably crossed across the other, a book open at his side.

Once again, shock washed over me. Once again, my heart was broken. Bill O'Malley was only sixty-four years old.

We held a graveside service two days later, on the second anniversary of Ryan's death. In my eulogy, I expressed my thoughts:

> In thinking about him, I'm aware of the many contrasts that made him who he was. He was a man who experienced a great deal of loss in his life, but also joy. He had a profound sense of sadness about him that was cared for by a marvelous sense of humor. He often stated his preference for being alone, yet would talk for hours with those who would listen. He would be tearful and speechless when those he cared about were in pain.
>
> It seemed that in the last few years he did find what he wanted: a very simple, unencumbered lifestyle with a few close friends and a lot of time—time to spend with his children and their spouses and his grandsons and time to be alone, to read, and fish and think.

Our son's grave was just outside the burial tent at the cemetery. After the service, we paused there on the way to the car. It just seemed unreal to be there again, first and third generations buried twenty yards apart, sorrow on top of sorrow.

Just that quickly I had crashed from the mountaintop of new fatherhood to the familiar dark place where I had lived for so much of the time since Ryan's death. Caring for little Kevan took some sting out of the sadness that distracted me, but for another long summer, I lived in a large pool of sorrow. I felt tugged in two directions, between birth and death; joy and sadness were separated only by a heartbeat.

After my father's death, I took two weeks off from work, having learned from Ryan's death that taking more time was better. I tended to Dad's estate and rested. I held Nancy and Kevan close. And then it was time to return to the world.

2

THE CAGE OF THE STAGES

One morning in 2007, glancing at my local newspaper before work, I was stunned to come across this headline: "Study Confirms Five Stages of Grief." The accompanying article began, "When a loved one dies, people go through five stages of grieving, according to accepted wisdom . . . Now the first large-scale study to examine the five stages shows not only that they are accurate, but also that people who have not reached the acceptance stage by six months may need professional help."[1]

As I read, disbelief washed over me—then anger. I knew better by then, because of my own clinical experience with more than a thousand grieving people for nearly three decades. I had believed in the stages once and had attempted to use them to diagnose my own grief and the grief of bereaved people who sought me out. But in case after case, I looked for so-called denial in my clients and found none. Time after time, grieving people sat in my office and told me they were perplexed by their lack of "anger." Me, too. After Ryan's death, I felt a lot of things, but anger wasn't one of them. "Bargaining"—what was that? Most of the grieving people I saw weren't "depressed"; they were just deeply and understandably sad. And "acceptance"? If that meant clients eventually returned to feeling as they had before their loss, that was not what I observed.

That's why, by 2007, like an increasing number of others in my field, I had been encouraging my clients to not feel confined by the stages of grief. I did not believe that those stages conformed to real life, at least not in the rigid, lockstep way in which they were commonly understood.

I also came to learn another important lesson from my experience—theories like the stages were actually damaging to the bereaved. They placed people like Mary from the introduction in a box; they established an artificial and unreasonable timeline for suffering. In addition to the original pain of loss, the bereaved suffered from self-doubt, self-criticism, and shame when their experiences did not comply with the accepted wisdom.

On that morning in 2007, I saw that flawed and damaging orthodoxy seemingly being endorsed and legitimized at the highest levels of my profession. The newspaper story—a version of which was printed in papers across the nation—was based on an article in the esteemed *Journal of the American Medical Association*. That article, in turn, was based on results of research at Yale University.

I immediately put down my paper and went to my computer. I found the journal article and other published accounts of the study and tried to figure out just how the researchers had reached their conclusions. As it turned out, the article was based on a study of 233 grieving people, a significant enough number. But to my mind, many problems were immediately evident.

First, the studied population was dominated by one subgroup: elderly people who had lost a spouse. Thus, it was misleading to suggest that the study represented a broader grieving population. Others, such as those who had suffered a traumatic loss, were eliminated as subjects, though why was never made clear.

I knew firsthand that the experiences of people in that category tended to be much more complicated and less predictable.

Second, and most important in my mind, the research did not aspire to test the validity of the stages model. In fact, the study assumed the stages to be true. The purpose of the research was to study the stages in the subjects over time, not to challenge the stages themselves. It was another misguided attempt to quantify the unquantifiable, which was the problem with the stages of grief to start with.

But the damage was done. Forty years after Elisabeth Kübler-Ross introduced the stages of grief in *On Death and Dying,* grievers were again being told how they should feel and for how long. If they didn't follow the stages, then the experts said they might be suffering from a mental health disorder that should be treated by a professional.

Over the years, my grieving clients have come to see me for two reasons above all. First, given our death-phobic society, they felt like they had no other safe place to share the true feelings about their loss. Second, they were worried that they were going crazy. That concern was largely the by-product of theories like the stages of grief, which attempt to take a phenomenon that is natural, wholly unique, and unpredictable and make it into something diagnosable, like tonsillitis.

Hard as it is to conceive now, there was a time when humans lived without the benefit of mental health professionals to pronounce whether they were grieving correctly. The idea of "grieving correctly" would have seemed a ludicrous notion centuries ago, in the days before antibiotics and vaccines, when death was so much a part of everyday life. Most people lived on farms or in small towns and relied on their neighbors for consoling food and emotional support. The corpse was laid out in the family living room before the procession to church and cemetery. I have no doubt that the sorrow of those times was as deep as anything we experience today, but I also think there may have been something more natural about it all.

Then came the Industrial Revolution and the migration from country to city. People left behind their tight-knit communities and found themselves increasingly isolated in the anonymous crush of urban life. The assembly line did not stop for grief. Funeral homes came into being to provide living rooms for rent. With advances in medicine, we started living longer. With each passing decade, death became more foreign and unnatural.

The same thing happened with grieving. Community life and associated rituals of support for the bereaved began to disappear. In the past few decades, with the decline of organized religion as a unifying center of the community and a source of comfort, the isolation has grown ever more pronounced.

Psychology stepped into this profound human void, attempting to fill what the absence of the community and religion left for the individual to manage alone. If, to a significant degree, a goal of my profession is to alleviate suffering, what was a more universally painful experience than loss? But a person's grief experience gradually became a data point, something to be studied and dissected. We tried to put mourning under a figurative microscope, tried to fit it into a "medical model" as an illness to treat, not as a normal and inevitable phenomenon of life.

Sigmund Freud was among the first to weigh in on this phenomenon. In his famous 1917 paper "Mourning and

Melancholia," the father of modern psychology attempted to make the distinction between mourning and depression (or what he called melancholia).[2] Though the symptoms were similar, Freud held that mourning, triggered by the loss of a loved one, was normal, healthy, and temporary. He theorized that when mourning was done, the bereaved person would be free from the emotional attachment to the deceased. "[W]hen the work of mourning is completed the ego becomes free and uninhibited again," he wrote.[3]

Two words in Freud's statement—*work* and *completed*—laid the foundation for so much of what was to come in the following decades of grief theory. His paper was also the birth of the notion of grieving as a process—with a beginning, a middle, and an end.

But even Freud's own experience did not seem to bear this theory out. Nine years after the death of his daughter, on what would have been her thirty-sixth birthday, Freud wrote to his friend Ludwig Binswanger, who had just lost his own son:

> Although we know that after such a loss the acute state of mourning will subside, we also know we shall remain inconsolable and will never find a substitute. No matter what may fill the gap, even if it be filled completely, it nevertheless remains something else. And actually this is how it should be. It is the only way of perpetuating the love we do not want to relinquish.[4]

Another milestone in the study of grief came during World War II, with the work of a psychiatrist named Erich Lindemann. In 1942, nearly five hundred people perished in a fire at Boston's Cocoanut Grove nightclub, the worst disaster of its kind in American history. In the aftermath, Lindemann, chief of psychiatry at Boston

General Hospital, undertook the first systematic study of grief by interviewing the survivors of the dead.

Taking a page from Freud, Lindemann coined the term *grief work*. His work tracked Freud's in other important ways, particularly with regards to the notion that the outcome of completed grief work was detachment, or a withdrawal of emotion, energy, and feelings for the deceased. He wrote, "The duration of a grief reaction seems to depend upon the success with which a person does the *grief work*, namely, emancipation from the bondage to the deceased, readjustment to the environment in which the deceased is missing, and the formation of new relationships."[5]

Lindemann, who influenced many theorists to come, was also the first to put grief on a strict timeline. He wrote that eight to ten sessions with a psychiatrist over a period of four to six weeks was sufficient to manage most cases of grieving. This idea still makes me cringe.

As the twentieth century unfolded, other psychological theories and schools of thought, which were created to treat maladies such as family dysfunction, addiction, and anxiety disorders, were retrofitted to tackle grief. A prominent example is a school of psychology in which I was trained, Gestalt. The goal of Gestalt theory and therapy, which came to prominence in the 1950s and 1960s, was to help a client resolve "unfinished business" from past relationships and traumas. Gestalt therapists were trained to put their clients through rituals and exercises, such as the empty chair and letter writing, to access and resolve old emotional wounds. But once again, the purpose was an end to pain, a completion of it, a task completed. Gestalt and other emerging schools offered techniques that endorsed more or less the same objectives—completion, detachment, and acceptance.

The grieving person who did not move beyond the pain of loss had failed somehow or was pathological, which is exactly how I felt for a long time after Ryan's death—as if something was wrong with me. The Gestalt therapist who had me talk to the empty chair assumed that I had gotten bogged down in my mission of letting go and that, consequently, I was "stuck" in my grief. In the excruciating months and years after Ryan's death, I assumed the same. I was determined to break through and achieve this Gestalt "closure."

The following story is an example of my commitment.

A few months after our loss, I attended a fall retreat with my colleagues. At the time, I was sleep deprived and weepy and thus clearly "behind" in my mourning. On the first afternoon of the retreat, after we had finished our work, I struck off alone on a path into the woods. A gurgling stream seemed to offer me an opportunity for resolution.

I picked up a small stick at the side of the water and decided that the twig would represent my son. I silently chanted that it was time to let go of Ryan, that it was time to accept his death. After some reflection and deep breathing, I bent and set the twig into the water, watching as it floated down the stream and finally out of sight. I stood by the water for several minutes, desiring catharsis, wishing for resolution. Nothing happened.

Elisabeth Kübler-Ross was a psychiatrist and a native of Switzerland. She married an American and moved to the United States in 1958. During her psychiatry residency in New York in the 1960s, she became interested in the treatment of the terminally ill in Western societies. Her groundbreaking study of the dying was the basis of her 1969 book, *On Death and Dying.*

"It is not meant to be a textbook on how to manage dying patients, nor is it intended as a complete study of the psychology of dying," she wrote in the book's preface. "It is simply an account of a new and challenging opportunity to refocus on the patient as a human being . . . We have asked him to be our teacher so that we may learn more about the final stages of life with all its anxieties, fears, and hopes."[6] Despite this opening caveat, Kübler-Ross went on to introduce the stages in authoritative, declarative sentences, as if they were fact, not an interesting theory:

> "Denial functions as a buffer after unexpected shocking news, allows the patient to collect himself and, with time, mobilize other, less radical defenses."[7]

> "When the first stage of denial cannot be maintained any longer, it is replaced by feelings of anger, rage, envy, and resentment. The logical next question becomes: 'Why me?'"[8]

> "The third stage, the stage of bargaining, is less well known but equally helpful to the patient, though only for brief periods of time. If we have been unable to face the sad facts in the first period and have been angry at people and God in the second phase, maybe we can succeed in entering into some sort of an agreement which may postpone the inevitable happening."[9]

> "When the terminally ill patient can no longer deny his illness, when he is forced to undergo more surgery or

hospitalization, when he begins to have more symptoms or becomes weaker and thinner, he cannot smile it off any more. His numbness or stoicism, his anger and rage will soon be replaced with a sense of great loss."[10]

"If a patient has had enough time . . . and has been given some help in working through the previously described stages, he will reach a stage during which he is neither depressed nor angry about his 'fate' . . . Acceptance should not be mistaken for a happy stage. It is almost void of feelings. It is as if the pain had gone, the struggle is over, and there comes a time for 'the final rest before the long journey' as one patient phrased it."[11]

Often lost is the fact that the aforementioned stages—even as they applied to dying people, not the bereaved—were met with skepticism.

In fact, three criticisms are summarized in the online reference *Encyclopedia of Death and Dying.* Chief among them is the relative flimsiness of Kübler-Ross's research, which "offered nothing beyond the authority of her clinical impressions and illustrations from selected examples to sustain this theory in its initial appearance."[12] Critics also argued that the stages were overly broad and thus could not adequately describe a complex emotional event like dying. Finally, the stages implied a sequential order to the emotional reality of dying, though even Kübler-Ross conceded that a person might move back and forth between stages.

Over the years, however, the skeptics were largely ignored. Because of their simplicity and apparent logic, the stages became a phenomenon. In my profession, it was only a small leap to apply them more broadly to those who were grieving the loss of another, in addition to those who were dying. We were eager to latch onto anything that might demystify the messy, confusing, and painful experience of mourning. It didn't hurt that Kübler-Ross seemed to endorse applying the stages more broadly. "Any natural, normal human being, when faced with any kind of loss, will go from shock all the way through acceptance," she said in 1981. "You could say the same about divorce, losing a job, a maid, a parakeet."[13]

With every passing year, as the stages became more ingrained as gospel, their application to the bereaved became more and more rigid. In the experience of mourning, the stages were not viewed as optional. "If you ignored or repressed the stages, you risked getting stuck with unresolved and painful emotions," Ruth Davis Konigsberg wrote in *The Truth About Grief: The Myth of Its Five Stages and the New Science of Loss.* "But if you plunged yourself through them, you would eventually emerge on the other side stronger and wiser, a reward that was particularly appealing in the 1970s as the self-help movement with its promise of personal transformation was sweeping the country."[14]

The stages of grief still remain the cultural orthodoxy. No psychological model has been imbedded as deeply in the popular culture as this one continues to be. Konigsberg called the Kübler-Ross model "the idea that wouldn't die." She described how the stages have permeated our culture, from politics to literature, and have become "a stock reference in popular entertainment, turning up in episodes of *Frasier* and *The Simpsons,* and more recently *The Office, Grey's Anatomy, Scrubs,* and *House.*"[15]

The stages are so prevalent that their mention tends to go in one ear and out the other—until we lose someone. For the bereaved, every reference to the five stages of grief on television or in the media can seem like a referendum on their own sorrow.

Take Suzanne, a young woman who came to see me a year after her brother-in-law had been killed in a workplace accident. Not only was Billy the man who had married her sister, but he and Suzanne had also been close friends since childhood. She was devastated by his death.

"He was like a brother to me," she told me.

But that was not what brought Suzanne to my office. A few weeks before we met, she had come across an article in a popular women's magazine that featured the stages of grief. In the article, several well-known therapists, citing the stages, suggested that a person should be concerned if their mourning had not begun to abate after six or seven months. The experts even had a term for it—*pathological grief*—and said it should be treated by a mental health professional.

It wasn't enough that Suzanne felt profound sorrow. She now wondered if she was pathological—sick, crazy—as well.

Another client, Nan, had recently lost her mother to cancer. She came to see me at a time when the stages had become accepted wisdom and self-diagnosis among grievers was epidemic. She got straight to the point on her first visit to my office: "I need closure," she said.

But she took her self-diagnosis to an even deeper level. Nan felt like she knew why she had not been able to achieve closure. It was the "repressed" anger she felt toward her dead mother.

"Tell me more about that," I said. "Do you know what you might be angry about?"

It turned out that Nan and her mother had had a highly complex and often painful relationship. The daughter had wanted to clear the air before her mother died but was repeatedly rebuffed by the dying woman.

"We had so much unfinished business," Nan told me, unknowingly using the old Gestalt term. "Now I have nowhere to go with these feelings. I'll live with this forever. My chance for closure is gone."

By the time I saw Nan, I thought differently about "unfinished business" and "closure" than I had in years past.

"You couldn't change your mother," I said. "Just like you can't change what you're feeling now."

"So what am I supposed to do?" she said. "I don't want to feel this way the rest of my life."

"Maybe it will help to know that almost no one achieves closure, at least not in the way you'd expect," I said. "Everyone's grief is different, but it's safe to say there is no finish line."

When I said that, there was an immediate change in her. She settled more deeply into her chair and sighed. Liberated from the rules and expectations of society, she could begin to relax. The biggest problem wasn't the complicated pain of her loss; it was the expectations society had placed on her and that she had placed on herself.

Multiply the experiences of Mary, Suzanne, and Nan by the millions. So much damage has been done by the theories and therapies promoting the ideas of finishing unfinished business and closure, the five stages chief among them. The words of this recent blog by Emily Eaton, a young mother whose son died from leukemia, are too familiar:

> [O]ne of the first things I did after I came out of my initial shock was ask a friend, "What are the 5 stages of grief, again?" I wanted a roadmap for my future. I wanted a to-do list. Then, I learned that the theory . . . is based neither on bereavement *nor* scientific research . . .

I wasn't just surprised. I was *disappointed*
when I learned the facts about Kübler-Ross's five
stages. I was mostly disappointed because I liked
the idea of having a map or path through this
process, which I could follow and track my progress
through a journey that by definition (I assumed)
had a beginning, middle, and end. But I was
also disappointed to learn that these five stages
had become conventional wisdom in the field of
psychology and mental health without any scientific
research to back it up.[16]

Megan Devine, a grief counselor and prominent advocate for
the bereaved, pointed out the flaws of the Kübler-Ross model in
a 2013 essay in the *Huffington Post*:

> [Kübler-Ross] identified five *common* experiences, not
> five *required* experiences. Her stages, whether applied to
> the dying or those left living, were meant to normalize
> and validate what someone *might* experience in the swirl
> of insanity that is loss and death and grief.
>
> The stages of grief were not meant to tell you what
> you feel, what you should feel, and when exactly you
> should feel it. They were not meant to dictate whether
> you are doing your grief "correctly" or not. They were
> meant to normalize a deeply not-normal time. They
> were meant to give comfort. Dr. Ross' work was meant
> as a kindness, not a cage.[17]

But a cage they have become.

≈

Strange as it seems today, my graduate counseling programs in the late 1970s didn't offer a single class on working with the bereaved. The grief research and theories I mentioned earlier remained obscure. That might be why Kübler-Ross's stages became such a phenomenon—they didn't have much competition.

I had only a casual knowledge of the stages at the time of Ryan's death, but I studied them much more deeply afterward. I had always been drawn to such models as they seemed to offer a formula for relieving pain. In the early 1980s, I still subscribed to the notion that with grief, resolution and closure were the goals, as they were for other psychological diagnoses. Resolution and closure were what the stages of grief seemed to promise.

I also needed a strategy for working with the bereaved, because after word got out about my own loss, I became known in my town as a grief expert, deservedly or not. A larger and larger percentage of my practice consisted of bereaved people, and the stages became the diagnostic lens through which I evaluated them.

Janie came to see me about two years after Ryan's death and six months after she had lost her own four-year-old son, Marcus. She had devoted her life to caring for the boy, who had suffered from a degenerative lung disease (though it was an unrelated infection from a hospital stay that had taken his life).

"I feel like I should be better by now," she told me in our first session. "I'm still depressed."

"That's a stage of grief," I told her.

I encouraged her to read Kübler-Ross. She did, finishing *On Death and Dying* by our next session and eager to discuss the stages. We went through them one by one.

"I guess I was in denial," she told me. "I always knew that Marcus could die from his lung condition, but for a long time I couldn't believe that it was something else entirely that caused his death."

Bargaining was never an issue, she said; nor was anger. In fact, Janie worried that there was something wrong with her because she wasn't angrier.

"That's just not my way," she said.

The one stage she could really relate to was depression—the lack of energy and constant tearfulness. That was what we focused on as I tried to move her along to acceptance. I employed the old Gestalt exercises: She talked to Marcus in the empty chair. She wrote her little boy beautiful, heartbreaking letters. In the six months that I saw her, almost every session was deeply emotional.

I have no doubt that Janie benefited from our time together. As is typical, by the time she came to see me, she wasn't comfortable talking about Marcus with her friends, many of whom were young mothers themselves. My office was a safe place for her. I also helped Janie and her husband understand the stresses that grief imposes on a marriage, and I suggested healthy ways for them to communicate about their loss.

But, after our last session, she was still deeply bereaved. I believed that my task had been to help her achieve some measurable change in her emotional state, some sense of resolution, and, in that regard, I seemed to have failed.

"Am I doing something wrong?" she asked me on one of our last visits.

I assured her that she was not.

"So how long will this take?"

I fumbled for a reply.

"Try to be patient," I said.

Then I confessed, "I don't think I've gotten there either."

Looking back, I don't know if I would have come to doubt the stages had I not been a grieving person myself and seen that they did not match up with my own experience. I was increasingly haunted by the notion that I was promoting a theory about loss that wasn't true in my own life. The words of my mentor echoed in my mind: "You should never expect something of a client you would not expect of yourself." I was caught in a curious limbo between doubting myself and doubting the ever-popular grief model.

I hoped that the answer could be found in more study or another theory. By the mid-1980s, there was no shortage of literature, because grief counseling was becoming an increasingly popular subspecialty of psychology. So, I read everything I could find.

Although the terms were often interchangeable, everything I found was a variation on the same theme—grief as work to reach an emotional conclusion. William Worden's *Grief Counseling and Grief Therapy,* the bible in my field, was a prominent example.[18] Worden described the four "tasks" of grieving: "Accept the Reality of the Loss," "Experience the Pain of the Loss," "Adjust to an Environment in Which the Deceased Is Missing," and "Withdraw Emotional Energy and Reinvest It in Another Relationship." (Worden has since changed the wording of his last task, but this is how it was stated when I learned it.)

The echoes of Freud, Lindemann, and Kübler-Ross were unmistakable. Grieving was predictable, the theorists said. Grievers could feel better if they just worked hard enough. There was something wrong with those who continued to suffer.

Most modern grief theories continue to promote the idea that pain of loss should come to an end. That is what is implied by the words *closure, acceptance, recovery,* and *resolution.* Closure advocates accuse those of us in the other camp of being enablers who encourage people to remain "stuck" in their grief or to "wallow." But we know what we have observed in the real world, and we have seen the pain that arbitrary models have caused in so many grieving people. And yet the stages and other resolution-based models still dominate our culture.

In the mid- to late-1980s, I realized it was time for me to find a new way—a new way to grieve and to help others who were grieving.

3

THE WAY FORWARD
THROUGH STORIES

The year was 1986. I had grave doubts about the stages of grief but had yet to turn my back on them completely. I had nothing else to fall back on, was groping around for a way to help my grieving clients, and was still trying to come to terms with my own lingering heartache.

Scott was a turning point.

At the time, it was a rare guy courageous enough to consult a shrink, and Scott was a strapping, thirty-five-year-old construction worker. He and his father had worked side by side in the family business for eighteen years; that partnership ended the day the older man suffered a fatal heart attack. Six months later, Scott came to see me at his wife's urging. When he sat down in my office, he looked like he would rather have a root canal. I'm sure he thought I would light incense and break into a chant.

"Dad would turn over in his grave," he said. "My wife and pastor said I should come. It wasn't my idea."

"Why do they think you need to be here?" I said.

"My wife says I'm irritable and drinking too much," he said. "They both say they're worried about me."

"Do they have reason to be?" I said.

"I don't think so," he said. "But I have been hitting the bottle a little too hard since Dad died. And I'm not very focused at work."

"I get it," I said. "But we won't go forward if you don't want to, unless you're open to at least giving this a shot."

"That's fair enough, I guess," he said.

Although I had serious doubts about the stages of grief, I thought there was a chance Scott might be able to relate to them, like a blueprint on a construction site.

"People tend to go through stages when they've had a loss," I said, listing them. "You might be dealing with some anger and depression. That's pretty normal. We could try to figure out where you are with that."

Scott didn't bite.

"Sounds like mumbo jumbo," he said.

"Come to think of it, maybe it is," I said.

"So now what?"

"You said your dad would turn over in his grave," I said. "Why is that?"

"He was one tough fella," he said. "You should have known him."

For the next forty-five minutes, he spoke nonstop.

"He came from hard times. Nobody ever gave him anything," Scott said. "But from the time he was a kid, he wanted to own a business—and sure enough, he built ours with his own sweat and blood."

Scott's dad was his Little League coach. He taught his son how to hunt and fish.

"In high school, I got caught stealing some beer," Scott said. "My dad let me sit in jail that night. The next morning, he put me out with the guys unloading cement bags from a boxcar. For a month he made me sweep floors and clean the toilets at the office. He never said two words to me the whole time.

"Then one day he comes and says, 'It's about time you decide whether you're going to be a man or a thug.'"

"So you chose," I said.

"I chose," he said. "The beer was never mentioned again."

I was torn as I listened. I felt a little inadequate because I hadn't persuaded him that the stages might be useful. I was still looking for clues about where Scott was with his grief. I was tempted to interrupt him, to guide him back to his "grief work." It was my job, after all, to get him less impatient, less angry, and to curtail the alcohol. It occurred to me that Scott was trying to avoid his feelings by telling me his story, but he would not be deterred. I had no real choice but to sit back and let him talk. He was a natural storyteller and seemed to gather momentum as the minutes ticked by.

"I'm sorry," I said finally. "We're out of time."

He seemed disappointed.

"We could finish the next time," I said. "That is, if you want to come back."

"I guess I could," he said.

A week later Scott picked up where he left off. He remembered how after high school, he decided to go work for his dad.

"One day ten years later, he called me into his office," Scott said. "I wondered what I had done this time. Instead he said, 'It's about time you take your proper place here. From now on, you and I will be co-owners.' He shook my hand and told me to get back to work. It was the proudest day of my life."

Scott and his dad had their share of arguments but always resolved them.

"We were always competing," Scott told me, a wistful smile on his face. "Shooting the deer with the biggest rack. Catching the biggest fish. Betting on football and basketball games. The loser had to buy the first beer the next time we were in the bar. But he never kept track. He always bought the first one."

"And I remember how he was always so patient with customers," Scott said. "As tough as he was, he had really good people skills. The customer was always right, even though many times they were just plain wrong. He and I would argue about that. I wanted to charge more when people made unreasonable demands or changed their minds about a paint color. My dad reminded me that the next job might come from the last one. 'A positive recommendation was more important than proving a customer wrong.'"

Then Scott paused, seeming to brace himself for what came next. The telephone call. The emergency room.

"He was gone by the time I got there," Scott said. "He was laying there with these wires attached to him. His eyes were closed. But that wasn't my dad. He was up with the sun every day and could outwork ten men and now . . . nothing. I felt the room start to spin, but I had to snap out of it because my mother was holding onto my arm and she was a basket case. I had to keep it together for her. I've always had to keep it together."

Finally, Scott couldn't talk at all because of his weeping. I thought, "There are no theories or diagnoses needed here. Scott is doing exactly what he needs to do."

Telling his story was his therapy.

Not long after I met Scott, I remembered a similar experience of my own, just a few weeks after Ryan's death. I had reached out to a locally respected pastoral counselor, a quiet, dignified gentleman about twenty years older than me. As we sat down, he told me how sorry he was for my loss. I thanked him but quickly came to my agenda. I wanted him to tell me how he thought I was doing with my grief. He gently steered me in another direction.

"Tell me about Ryan and we can go from there," he said. "Start wherever you'd like."

So I talked first about my son's precarious birth and six months in the hospital, followed by the joy of his homecoming and the devastation of his death. It was the first time I had told the story of Ryan from beginning to end to someone I didn't know. I didn't get more than a few words out before I began to cry.

The counselor said very little, just nodded and occasionally asked clarifying questions. I could feel his compassion in the power of his attention and presence, the empathy in his eyes and in his expression. Instead of theories or therapeutic interventions, he offered deep human connection—and affirmation. He told me I was doing fine with my grief.

I saw that kindly man three or four times and felt great comfort each time. It was such a blessing to have a place to speak so openly of Ryan, to express my sorrow in such a pure and uninhibited way. It was lovely to be listened to like that. But at the time, I minimized the benefits of our sessions because resolution—both for me as a grieving father and for my clients—had been the goal.

After Scott, however, I became less concerned with moving my clients to closure. More and more I found myself attempting to emulate that gentle counselor, trying to listen actively and with empathy. I was increasingly content to have clients lead me, not the other way around. I simply encouraged them to tell their stories.

Time after time, as the stories poured out, so did their pure feelings of sorrow and often of love and gratitude. It soon dawned on me that, through their stories, my clients were being liberated from external rules or expectations and thus could grieve in a much more natural way.

As I listened to my clients' stories, the following sort of questions naturally came up—questions that didn't interrupt the flow of the story but that naturally took it deeper in spots.

"What was it like for you the day he was born?"

"How did you meet?"

"Do you have a favorite memory?"

"When was she happiest?"

"What made him sad?"

"How did you learn your sister had died?"

"When was the last time you talked to your father?"

"What did it feel like to hold her hand when she died?"

I asked clients to bring photographs and keepsakes to stimulate their remembering. It was wonderful when a bereaved person could spend fifty minutes remembering just one Christmas. In the past, I would have considered all of it a waste of time, a distraction from "grief work." But no longer.

Over the years, the bereaved have typically come to see me when they believe they should be feeling better than they are after a loss—generally, six months to a year. In a sense, they come looking for a cure. No wonder some clients are skeptical, even disappointed, when I introduce them to my "story listening" method and suggest that their grief might not come to a predictable and efficient end. This is particularly true of those who come to see me soon after a traumatic loss of disorienting intensity.

Mary, who you met in the introduction, definitely wasn't there to tell her story; she was there to discuss her symptoms. In our first session, I asked her to put them aside and tell me about her infant daughter.

"How is that going to help me?" she asked.

"Trust me. It's just important for me to hear," I said.

She paused.

"Okay," she said finally. "Where do I start?"

"How about at the beginning," I said. "Start with your pregnancy."

"If you say so," she said.

Mary had been delighted to learn she was pregnant and had big dreams for the daughter she named Stephanie. Mary stayed home with her daughter for the first three months of Stephanie's life and later found a comfortable balance between motherhood and her busy life as a professional. Mary's full day included feeding Stephanie before work, then bathing and feeding her at night, and rocking her to sleep with classical music playing softly in the background. That last one was a moment that Mary looked forward to all day.

"That first smile," she said. "If I live to be a hundred, I won't forget it. We were in her nursery. I had just changed her diaper; as I bent over to kiss her forehead, there it was. At first I thought I was imagining it, but I could see it in her eyes. She didn't have the words to say it, but my little girl loved me as much as I loved her."

Mary paused, working up to what she wanted to tell me next.

"It was a Saturday, a beautiful fall day. I had put Stephanie in the stroller for a walk around the block. I fed her when we got home and put her down for her usual nap. My husband was watching football. I thumbed through a magazine and dozed off myself. It wasn't an hour after I laid her down that I went to peek in on her. I could tell something was wrong. Her color was off. I screamed for my husband. When he got there, we realized she wasn't breathing."

Mary's hands were shaking as she rubbed her eyes, trying to fight off tears. So much of what she described next was achingly familiar—beginning CPR while her husband called for help; surrendering her daughter to an emergency crew; the drive behind the ambulance to the hospital. She described the hospital waiting room down to the furniture's color.

"My husband and I were sitting there, staring at the door, and finally it swung open," she said. "There was another man with our doctor. He introduced himself as the hospital chaplain. That's when I knew."

"We ended up in another room," she continued. "I don't even know how we got there. But the chaplain reached down into the little crib and handed Stephanie to me."

That's when Mary's defenses crumbled and she began to sob. The intensity of her pent-up emotions took her breath away and seemed to frighten her.

"You're fine," I said. "Just try to breathe. Take your time."

"It's still like a dream. It doesn't seem real," she said when the spasms of sadness had run their course. She slumped in her chair. "I didn't think it was possible to love so much. And just like that . . . What a cruel world!"

I nodded.

"Now what?" she said.

"You don't need to know the answer to that right now," I said.

"I've never talked about what happened, at least not like this, the whole story," she said. "I've never cried like that, either."

"I think it's good that you did," I said.

"It's funny, but it seems that I love Stephanie as much right now as the day she was born," Mary said as more tears spilled down her cheek. "But what's wrong with me. It's been six months. Why am I so sad?"

"I think you just answered that question yourself," I said.

"What do you mean?"

"You're sad because of how much you love your daughter. Your feelings are exactly as they are meant to be. You're not stuck. You're not depressed. You're not behind in your grief. You are mourning because you loved her."

"My precious Stephanie. I'll always miss her."

"I'll always miss my little boy," I said. "I don't think we want that to end."

Mary pondered that for a moment.

"No, we don't," she said.

In the months to come, Mary more deeply embraced her narrative of grief and the feelings that came with it. Each session brought new memories—some of them joyful, others agonizing. She said she was still deeply sad but felt less tired. She joined a support group. She was still a hard-charging, upbeat professional, but at my suggestion, she took time each day to connect with her daughter—to look at photographs, touch Stephanie's blanket, and let the feelings come as they may.

The relief, the liberation, the love I saw in Mary became so common in my office. Gone was the performance-based grief work that promised resolution but that generally produced only frustration and more pain. By turning to stories instead, clients could experience their lives without the fear that they were going crazy.

"This is how it's supposed to go for you," I would tell them. "Let's just see where you are."

That reassurance was often all a person needed. I might never see a client again after that watershed moment. There is no question that when closure or resolution was no longer the goal, when clients were convinced they were not getting their grief wrong, their need for therapy abated or disappeared altogether.

Clients who had suffered a particularly traumatic loss tended to stay in therapy longer. (More on that in a later chapter.) Others continued to find my office the only safe place for their stories to be told and listened to. I worked with grieving children for more than thirty years. Many of the youngsters I saw at the ages of six through twelve would come back as teenagers or even as adults to update their stories with evolved language and new questions. As they reached new life stages, it was natural for them to wonder, as I did with Ryan, how their lives would have been different had their loved ones lived.

Many adults also return to my office to bring me into the current realities of their loss narrative. Some need reassurance that a surge of pain years later is normal. Some need to discuss life events, remarriage, or new losses.

When loss is a story and there is a safe place to tell it, a lovely bond develops between the teller of the story and the one who receives the story. I am always appreciative and humbled by the fact that so many clients come back years—or even decades—after their initial loss to ask for my help in reconnecting with their ongoing story.

≋

My practice thus evolved from one of a grieving therapist who promoted modern grief theories to one of a grieving therapist/companion/listener/story encourager. It's not an exaggeration to say that, over time, my clients and I redefined the nature of "successful" grieving. Grief wasn't getting over loss; it was learning to live with it and to use the grief narrative as a way to preserve a bond with the one who died. My clients made the liberating shift from thinking we *must* be angry or depressed or in denial to accepting that we *may* have those experiences.

If that liberation could come for my clients, I realized that it would also come for me. Through my clients' narratives of grief, I slowly opened up to a deeper appreciation and embrace of my own. It was like I became the gentle narrator of the story of Ryan's loss, rather than the suspicious mental health professional diagnosing a potential problem. As had been the case with my clients, embracing my story didn't remove my suffering; instead, it transformed it, made it more pure and simple by removing the fear that I was doing it wrong.

I was free to observe my feelings, day by day, without shame or judgment and without trying to fit them into a theory. Once my interior monologue might have gone like this: "I'm sad today. It's been more than a year. That seems excessive. What's wrong with me?" After I relaxed into my story, this is more likely how it would go: "Ryan would have been thirty-six in two months. I'm sad he is not here."

All the labeling and analysis implied that my sadness was a symptom. But it wasn't. Once I might have asked myself, "I'm happy today. Does that mean I'm not missing him? Am I repressing my loss? How can I be happy when he's not here?" That became, "I'll always miss my son, but it feels great to laugh again."

Finally, I realized that all the analysis was competing for space with my love. When I stopped judging my mourning, so much love, intimacy, and grace flowed back into my heart. There was so much bittersweet joy in reconnecting to the love.

This moment was almost always the turning point for my clients as well—the moment when they came to understand that their grief was a function of their love. Who could argue with that? How could there be shame in their sorrow? How could their feelings be wrong? How could their feelings do anything but connect them with the ones they missed? The feelings, painful as they might be, were honoring. They were affirming. Grief could be something to be grateful for.

Once I had been haunted by these questions: What's wrong with my clients? What's wrong with me? What a relief to realize that there was nothing wrong with any of us. We were not crazy. We were not wallowing.

Clients would ask, "How long will this take?"

And I would reply, "How deeply did you love?"

Because of what I experienced with my clients and as a grieving father, I now subscribe to a school of thought that could not be more different from the prescriptive, achievement-oriented models. It is called "continuing bonds."

Continuing Bonds: New Understandings of Grief was published in 1996.[1] The authors, Dennis Klass, Phyllis R. Silverman, and Steven Nickman, were researchers and clinicians who realized that what they were hearing from grieving families and individuals in real settings was inconsistent with the modern grief models. They studied diaries of the bereaved from the nineteenth century, grieving rituals from other cultures, and the behavior of grieving and adopted children; they also interviewed bereaved parents in support groups. Their findings were similar to my own: in grievers, there was a pervasive and deep longing for connection to the one they lost and great resistance to the idea of ending their emotional attachment to the deceased. They wrote:

> [W]e were observing phenomena that could not be accounted for within the models of grief that most of our colleagues were using. It appeared that what we were observing was not a stage of disengagement, which we were educated to expect, but rather, we were observing people altering and then continuing their relationship to the lost or dead person. Remaining connected seemed to facilitate both adults' and children's ability to cope with the loss and the accompanying changes in their lives. These "connections" provided solace, comfort and support and eased the transition from the past to the future.[2]

The idea of continuing bonds removes the imperative to "achieve closure," "get over," "move on," or "let go." That, in turn, lessens the shame that so many people feel when they think they are not getting grief right.

The authors noted, "While the intensity of the relationship with the deceased may diminish with time, the relationship does not disappear. We are not talking about living in the past, but rather recognizing how bonds formed in the past can inform our present and our future."[3]

Continuing bonds concedes the reality that the pain of loss is likely to linger in some form. The bereaved are thus encouraged to redefine, not end, their relationship with the deceased. It is not a how-to model like many theories; rather, it is more consistent with how humankind grieved before psychology and cultural forces co-opted the landscape.

The continuing bonds theory hasn't (yet) gained enough traction to supplant the popular stages or how-to models. But someday it will, and I hope this book is part of the return to a grieving that is more natural, authentic, and humane.

4

ON THE RIGHT PATH

When I turned away from the stages and grief-work theories and toward the narrative of grief, it felt as if I were practicing on a cultural and professional island. The only affirmation for my new way came from my clients, as I watched them shed their shame, which opened them to tears of love. Where once I referred grieving people to orderly models as a map for their loss journey, now I walked with them as I waited for outside confirmation that we were on the right path.

That confirmation came in the late 1980s, when I was creating a training program for volunteer facilitators at The WARM (What About Remembering Me) Place, a local center for bereaved children and their families. While gathering teaching material, I remembered a film I had seen several years before. Robert Redford's Oscar-winning *Ordinary People* (1980) was about a family torn apart by traumatic loss. As I watched it again after so many years, it felt like one of those "hidden in plain sight" experiences. My evolution as a therapist from stages to story could not have been more powerfully validated.

Rarely, in my experience, has art so faithfully portrayed real life. The movie lays utterly bare so many realities of grieving, such as how a husband and wife typically grieve so differently and the stress that the difference puts on a marriage. The crippling anguish of survivor's guilt is another.

The tragedy is a sailing accident involving two teenage brothers, Buck and Conrad, who are caught in a sudden storm. When their boat overturns, Buck slips from Conrad's grasp and drowns.

Timothy Hutton played the role of Conrad, who is consumed with feelings of self-blame and guilt to the extent that he attempts suicide. This attempt is what lands him in the office of his therapist, Dr. Berger, played by Judd Hirsch.

What most resonated with me in the movie was the relationship between Dr. Berger and Conrad. After much sparring between the two, the therapist's office becomes a safe place for his client. Conrad's story of loss and his profound guilt eventually come pouring out during one of their sessions.

"I'm scared," the boy says, starting to quietly weep.

"Feelings are scary," Dr. Berger says. "Sometimes they're painful. And if you can't feel pain, you're not going to feel anything else, either. You hear what I'm saying. You're here. You're alive. And don't tell me you don't feel that."

In the next scene, the light is back in Conrad's eyes. It was a light I recognized, one that I had seen so many times myself, when my clients felt safe enough to discard their self-judgment and simply tell their stories of loss. The fictional therapist in *Ordinary People* made no mention of theories, steps, or stages. He attempted instead to reach this young man through his presence, his ability to listen and create a safe place for Conrad's true story to emerge.

Ordinary People went far to assure me, to remove any lingering doubts about whether I was on the right path with my clients. I continue to recommend it to them. I've used the film to teach hundreds of volunteers at The WARM Place, stressing the importance of a caring person and of creating a place of safety for the suffering of another to be witnessed and received.

As a graduate student and young therapist, I conscientiously devoured the writings of giants of my field—from Freud to dozens of contemporary clinicians. I was always adding to my home library books about promising new theories that might help me alleviate the suffering of my grieving clients, as well as my own. But as the narrative of grief became more and more central to my practice, my reading habits changed as well. I was drawn to writers and poets who chose to explore, commemorate, and share their suffering through their craft.

I found authenticity there. The stories and poems were not written through the lens of what *should be* happening but what *was* happening. They were beautiful, soulful, and they seemed to cut to the core of the grief experience. These I also recommended to my clients.

I can only assume that Joan Didion, one of our most celebrated contemporary writers, was searching for meaning, not a bestseller, when she began to explore the death of her husband, John Gregory Dunne. Nonetheless, she more or less created a new literary genre with her 2005 book *The Year of Magical Thinking,* a memoir of loss.

Few of us have Didion's facility with the language, but all of us can learn from her honest, fearless, nonjudgmental self-observation:

> It is now, as I begin to write this, the afternoon of
> October 4, 2004. Nine months and five days ago, at
> approximately nine o'clock on the evening of December

30, 2003, my husband, John Gregory Dunne, appeared
to (or did) experience, at the table where he and I
had just sat down to dinner in the living room of our
apartment in New York, a sudden massive coronary
event that caused his death . . . This is my attempt to
make sense of the period that followed, weeks and then
months that cut loose any fixed idea I ever had about
death, about illness, about probability and luck, about
good fortune and bad, about marriage and children and
memory, about grief, about the ways in which people do
and do not deal with the fact that life ends, about the
shallowness of sanity, about life itself.[1]

She described the hours before and after her husband's death
in that telling, writerly detail. As they will in your story, those
details, so mundane before, took on haunting significance.

I got him a Scotch and gave it to him in the living room,
where he was reading in the chair by the fire where he
habitually sat . . .

I finished getting dinner. I set the table in the living
room where, when we were home alone, we could eat in
sight of the fire . . .

John asked for a second drink before sitting down.
I gave it to him. We sat down. My attention was on
mixing the salad.

John was talking, then he wasn't . . .

I only remember looking up. His left hand was raised
and he was slumped motionless.[2]

She wrote about how, in the months to come, she could not give
away some of her husband's clothing, in the "magical" belief

that he would someday return. She excavated favorite memories, like the time he read her a passage from one of her own novels. Their times apart when they racked up huge long-distance telephone bills. The short white silk dress she wore to their wedding. The navy blue suit he wore for the occasion.

And this: "I know why we try to keep the dead alive: we try to keep them alive in order to keep them with us."[3]

Another book I recommend to my clients is Meghan O'Rourke's *The Long Goodbye*, a memoir about the death of her mother. O'Rourke, a critic and poet, began writing about her experience of loss in the early days after her mother's death. Her narrative is from a poet's heart and is completely devoid of clinical analysis.

> In the weeks after my mother's death, I experienced
> an acute nostalgia. This longing for a lost time was
> so intense I thought it might split me right in two,
> like a tree hit by lightning. I was—as the expression
> goes—flooded by memories. It was a submersion in
> the past that threatened to overwhelm any "rational"
> experience in the present, water coming up around my
> branches, rising higher. I did not care much about work
> I had to do. I was consumed by memories of seemingly
> trivial things.[4]

O'Rourke and I agree on the ultimate reality of grief, though she expresses it more elegantly that I ever could.

> I was thinking about how hard it was to say how much I
> missed my mother, yet how central the feeling was. It is
> heartsickness, like the sadness you feel after a breakup, but
> many times stronger and more desperate. I miss her: I want

to talk to her, hear her voice, have a joke with her. I am willing for us to be "broken up" if she'll just have dinner with me once. *And as I was walking I thought: "I will carry this wound forever." It's not a question of getting over it or healing. No; it's a question of learning to live with this transformation. For the loss is transformative, in good ways and bad, a tangle of change that cannot be threaded into the usual narrative spools. It is too central for that. It's not an emergence from the cocoon, but a tree growing around an obstruction.*[5] (Italics added.)

Scott Simon, an award-winning journalist and host of National Public Radio's *Weekend Edition Saturday,* first told the story of his mother's dying and death in a series of Twitter posts. The tweets, which went viral, were poignant, humorous, lyrical, and full of grace.

That moment-by-moment sharing on social media inspired not only much praise and support but also some criticism. In his memoir, *Unforgettable,* he explained why he had felt it was important to tell his story:

> I hadn't implied—and this was important to her—that my mother's death was any kind of tragedy. She had lived a long full, and rewarding life, and then she died. I posted messages in which I confided some of my fears, and shared some of my mother's sagacity and wit as we went through what is, after all, a universal experience.
>
> My mother died and I mourned. That's as much a part of life as love and taxes. Why be quiet about it? . . .
>
> Life-changing experiences can transform and teach us and move us to share what we believe we've learned. We want to . . . place the face of someone we've loved and

lost in the stars. We want people to know. It is an utterly human response, imperfect but invaluable.[6]

Finally, I've read and reread Edward Hirsch's book-length poem, *Gabriel,* dozens of times, finding my own feelings and experience in it. Gabriel is the name of Hirsch's dead son. The following passage always speaks to me:

> I did not know the work of mourning
> Is like carrying a bag of cement
> Up a mountain at night.
>
> The mountaintop is not in sight
> Because there is no mountaintop
> Poor Sisyphus grief
>
> I did not know I would struggle
> Through a ragged underbrush
> Without an upward path
>
> Because there is no path
> There is only a blunt rock
> With a river to fall into[7]

The words and stories of my clients, though perhaps less artfully told, were no less compelling.

Over the years, I've been gratified and delighted to discover a number of kindred spirits—professionals who share my belief in the importance and healing power of stories.

One is Dr. Candi Cann, a professor of world cultures and religions at Baylor University, who specializes in the study of death and human rituals of mourning. She is also the author of *Virtual Afterlives: Grieving the Dead in the Twenty-First Century.*[8] I was struck initially by a magazine essay in which she wrote that we tell our stories "as a way to piece together our narratives of bereavement and to remember those we love. Stories keep the dead in our lives, help make sense of their deaths, and communicate our losses to others. Narratives order lives in a timeline that we can recount and to which we can give meaning."[9]

She was kind enough to elaborate in a recent conversation with my coauthor:

> Part of what I've noticed about narrative-making is that the maker is creating their place with the dead, and putting that person in time, creating a place in history for them. I think that's really important. They construct meaning. These timelines are a way of sorting through and sifting through everything, so we can say, "Here is the high point. Here is the purpose." Some of it is artificial and very false, but some of it is valuable.[10]

Furthermore, she said, grief narratives push back against the dictates of a death-phobic society in which people no longer know how to mourn.

> There needs to be a counternarrative to society's overarching belief that we're supposed to "get over" people we've lost. We're supposed to stop grieving and move on . . . I just don't agree with that. The grief story allows people to have a voice that society is trying to either ignore or silence.

Grief will make itself heard, no matter what. It may be in pathological ways, because it's been suppressed for years. Grief storytelling is particularly important because when we embrace grief and these stories, we also embrace the fragility of life. These are things that our society, with the tempo of our times, encourages us to ignore.

Death is a part of life. This is the whole thing, an everyday part of life. I tell people that when you give birth to a child, you also give birth to them dying someday. We just have to accept that.[11]

I had heard of the narrative medicine movement for years, but it was not until my research for this book that I sought out its founder, Dr. Rita Charon. The author of *Narrative Medicine: Honoring the Stories of Illness,* she is a kindred spirit, indeed.[12]

The daughter of a physician, Charon had also been a voracious reader as a child. When she began to practice medicine herself, as an internist at a clinic in an impoverished New York City neighborhood, she soon realized how her early passion for literature was also central to her life's work as a medical healer. As she explained in a 2011 TEDxAtlanta talk,

> What patients paid me to do was to pay exquisite attention to the narratives they gave me, which were in words, in silences, in those facial expressions, . . . in the tracings and pictures that we had of their body, in what other people said about them. And it was my task to cohere these stories, so they at least provisionally made some sense; to take these multiple, contradictory

narratives and let them build something that we could act on. So that's what we did.[13]

Inspired by her belief that she could better serve her patients by understanding stories and how they were told, Charon went on to earn a master's degree and PhD in English literature from Columbia University. She then founded the narrative medicine program at Columbia's medical school, which has been emulated in many others, and she lectures around the world on the topic.

> What I learned, right from the beginning, was
> that persons were not only able but deeply thirsty
> to give profound, detailed, eloquent accounts of
> themselves. They didn't always know how to start.
> One woman said, "You want me to talk?" Another
> man . . . started to tell me about the death of his
> father, and then the death of his brother, and then
> the trouble he was having with his teenage son.
> And then he starts to cry. I broke my silence, and
> I said, "Why do you weep?" He says, "No one
> ever let me do this before."[14]

So how could the embrace of the story, the creativity, help grieving people? The question was put to Dr. Charon by my coauthor in a recent conversation.[15] She responded by recalling a primary loss in her own life:

> I could describe my father's death with dates and
> times, what medicines he was on, who was with him
> when he died . . . That's one way I could tell the
> story. I could also tell the story of my father's death
> by starting with my very first memory of him, when

I was a year and a half old and he was in the Army. He had me on his shoulder because we were at St. Peter's Square at the Vatican. That's very different, isn't it?

When I say *creative writing,* I mean writing for discovery. If I was not trying to write creatively, I might not have remembered this experience of being a year and a half old. I would not have known that was going to come to mind. And what comes to pen is not always what comes even to mind. People read what they have written, and they say, "I had no idea I was going to write that." This is standard. That's the kind of writing that would help people in grieving or anything else.

On that point, Dr. Charon and I certainly agree. She continued with her explanation:

In a way, [this kind of writing is] not really about grief; it's about life, whether someone lost a loved one or not . . . It's about experiencing one's present and past deeply. I can see how it could be useful for grief, but I can imagine it could be useful for a lot of other things, like loneliness or feeling embittered or just plain old depression . . . Grief is just one of the potential applications.

The practice of listening to patient/client stories . . . is one of deepening that nurse or social worker or chaplain or physician, so that that person can see, can perceive, and then [can] appropriately respond to what the client or patient is going through.

According to Charon, this practice enlarges our "capacity to witness life." She went on to explain, "Some of the doctors I train [in narrative medicine], I ask them afterward, 'Has this changed your teaching? Has what you've learned changed your practice in pediatrics?' One of them said, 'Come on. This has made me a better father.'"

The examples of grief narratives in literature and film showed me not only that I was on the right track by encouraging my clients to tell their stories of grief, but also that telling these stories is a deeply human, instinctual need. The insights offered by Cann and Charon began to explain why. We are all, as Charon says, "deeply thirsty to give profound, detailed, eloquent accounts" of ourselves. Because few stories involve only a single "character," our accounts of ourselves must naturally incorporate the other people in our lives, including those we have lost. Indeed, the story of loving and losing someone is a classic human story, as storytellers have been reminding us for centuries. Letting go of the idea of stages, grief work, and other psychological methods frees us to meet our grief in a way that I believe is organic, as well as truly valuable.

5

NO PERSON'S GRIEF THE SAME

We will take up your grief story in chapter 9. But before we do, it's important to understand why your narrative will be unlike that of any other human who has ever lived, like a fingerprint or a snowflake. The following list of factors, by no means exhaustive, will be explored more deeply in this chapter and the three to follow.

Environmental triggers This is the term for the people, places, things, scents, and tastes that remind you of the person you lost. You knew your loved one in a physical environment through your senses. A feeling will be associated with every reminder, and no person's environment is the same.

Personality and character differences Each of you is a unique confluence of nature, nurture, and life experiences, with no two humans designed alike. It follows that every person experiences loss and grief in his or her own way, according to their own unique way of being.

The circumstances of death Suicide, murder, sudden death by accident, or catastrophic health events like strokes or heart attacks introduce trauma, fear, and mental chaos to grieving. The aftermath of such a loss—so-called *interruptive death*—tends to be accompanied by much more intense experiences and feelings, as compared with the peaceful death of a loved one after a life well lived.

Attachment (or lack thereof) to the deceased In my experience, this is the most important factor. I've even developed an equation of sorts: the intensity and duration of your grief depends on your level of attachment to the person you lost. Put simply, what was your relationship to the deceased? How much did you love him or her, and why? Conversely, what was your level of discord or antagonism with the one who died? No two human relationships are the same.

These factors that explain the uniqueness of grief seem self-evident now, but it took me years of grieving and working with the bereaved before I connected the dots. My golden retriever, Lonigan, helped set me on the path of understanding.

It was a fine autumn Saturday in 1986, and I had spent much of the morning happily playing with Kevan and little Connor, our youngest child, who had been born the previous January. When I handed the boys off to their mother, I took up with a list of household chores. At the top was bathing the dog, whose veterinarian had prescribed a disinfectant soap for a skin infection.

I took Lonigan out back, hosed him down, and lathered him up, my mind no doubt on a thousand other things. But after a few seconds, I realized that I felt a surge of sadness and was unexplainably tearful. I sat down in the grass and tried to understand what was happening. The answer took a few seconds but eventually came to me. In the weeks and months after Ryan was born, before Nancy and I could touch or hold him in the intensive care unit, we needed to first scrub up with antiseptic soap. The scent of the soap I used with Lonigan was almost identical to that from the hospital.

That innocent sensory stimulus had cut straight to the place in my brain where the memories and feelings of Ryan would forever be stored. It is called the *limbic system,* a primitive part of our brain where human emotions are believed to be centered. A sight or smell might register there and is then interpreted and named by more advanced parts of our cognitive apparatus. The pungent aroma of antiseptic soap produced tears, which my brain could eventually link to the hospital.

For the grieving person (and for everyone else), this happens over and over. Smells, sights, or sounds are everywhere—triggers so pervasive and often so subtle that they are impossible to consciously be aware of or to guard against.

If this was true for me, I knew it had to be true for my grieving clients and for the bereaved everywhere. It also followed that every life, every environment is so different that no set of triggers could possibly be the same. Thus, how could every experience of mourning be the same?

Understanding the connection between grief and your environment often provides an important sanity check. Sudden, unexplainable shifts in feelings or states of mind can make a person feel unbalanced. Be assured, you are not losing your mind if the sight of his toothbrush brings tears to your eyes.

Or the sound of a stranger's laughter causes you to freeze. Or perhaps even silence in a moment when you anticipated sound. After all these years of listening to clients describe these types of triggers, I am still amazed at how subtle yet powerful these moments can be.

The following exercise is an inventory of your environment. In your journal, make a list of things in your daily life—sights, scents, sounds, people, and places—that remind you of the one you lost. These ideas will later become important elements in your story of loss.

- Did you share a favorite restaurant?

- Did he have a favorite toy? A favorite song? A favorite flower? A favorite sports team? A favorite season of the year?

- Are his books still in the bookcase as he arranged them?

- Can you still smell her scent in her closet?

- Are his golf clubs still in the garage?

- Are you aware of how quiet and empty the house now seems?

- What is your favorite photograph of the person you lost?

- What was it like the first time you went back to church after the funeral?

- What did you feel when you went through her clothes?

Add your own questions, based on your own environment and life with the one you lost. A hardware store, if you and your deceased father went there regularly for lawn fertilizer and garden tools, can be a powerful emotional trigger. The theme music of her favorite television show. The smell of laundry detergent.

When I took my own inventory, I recalled my first trip back to the hospital after Ryan was released. I was going to visit a friend who had just given birth. My stomach tumbled and my eyes welled the moment I stepped off the elevator into the maternity ward, which perplexed me at the time. But no wonder.

The transition from winter to spring has also always inspired melancholy. Springtime was when we finally brought Ryan home. Summer was my first season of anguish.

The autumn Ryan was born, Nancy had planted morning glories outside our home. The sight of those flowers will forever cause a moment's ache in my heart.

Eddie Rabbit's song "I Love a Rainy Night" was a hit the year of Ryan's birth. In the weeks after we had him home, I sang it to Ryan. I held him and danced. Tears come when I hear that silly song, even now.

A new dishwashing soap came out that spring when he was home, and that scent is forever connected with him. We still use that brand, and there is a twinge every time we clean the kitchen.

Every Saturday morning, on my way to meet a friend at a local diner for breakfast, I drive by the house where we lived when we brought Ryan home. When I pass by, I look at the porch where we sat to look at birds and butterflies, and I remember with a mixture of sadness, wonder, and gratitude.

Other children were also constant reminders. Several friends had kids Ryan's age, and I could not see them without longing for my son and trying to imagine him as a five- or six-year-old boy. That continues today, with something as innocuous as seeing a man in his mid-thirties with a son at a ballgame or rolling down the aisle at the supermarket. Ryan would likely be married and have a family of his own by now. I will forever mourn the fact that my son never had the chance.

For some reason, when the date of his birth or the date of his death line up with the day of the week when those events occurred, I find myself replaying every detail much more than I would otherwise. The mystery of triggers.

The inventory of your environment will probably be painful. It was for me. But breathe deep and reassure yourself that the feelings are okay. Sadness, confusion, anger, and yearning—no feeling is wrong. They all connect you to the one you lost.

Finally, try to be more aware of the triggers as you go through your day, reminding yourself that there is a reason tears come up or your breathing catches.

Helping my clients understand how environment affects mourning is a big part of my role as a grief therapist. In our first session, Brenda told me she felt like she was literally suffocating.

"Am I losing my mind?" she asked.

She wasn't.

Brenda and Fred had been married for ten years when he was killed in a traffic accident. They had begun each day sharing coffee before heading off to different jobs, but they spoke every few hours on the telephone. They trained dogs together, took dance lessons, enjoyed several favorite restaurants, and had all of the same friends. Except for her cubicle at work, there was not one physical space in Brenda's life that her husband did not share. Every place in their house, every step along the jogging trail, inspired yearning for her husband.

"You didn't love Fred in a bubble," I told her. "You loved him in a physical world full of sights, smells, sounds, and memories. That's why this is so intense all the time. You were never not together. Your lives were beautifully entwined."

Brenda was relieved she was not losing her mind. Normalizing this aspect of loss removes a great emotional burden. By understanding that reality of grieving, she could also make conscious choices about what to do with so much environmental stimuli. Brenda decided to remain in the home she and Fred had shared. To lose so many of the reminders of him would have seemed like another death. She could now embrace their shared world with a sense of peace, even when doing so was painful.

I also see people like Frank, a thirty-year-old man who came to me feeling confused and guilty. His concern was not feeling overwhelmed by the death of his father, but just the opposite. He was underwhelmed and wanted to know why.

At one time, I would have assumed he was repressing his feelings, and I would have put him through exercises to access them. But by the time he came to me, I had developed a different understanding.

Frank told me his parents had separated when he was three, and his dad had then moved to the West Coast. Frank didn't see his dad until his adolescent years and then only for a few weeks in the summer. Nor did Frank see his father much as an adult. Frank could go days without anything in his environment reminding him of his dead parent. Frank said he loved his father but shared very little time in the same space. Frank expected to feel more afflicted with sorrow, a cultural assumption of what a son should feel when his dad died; he was relieved that the absence of sadness did not mean he was an unfeeling person.

6

KNOW THYSELF

A re you the life of the party, or are you more comfortable in
a quiet corner with one or two friends?

Are you spontaneous or inclined to think things out
before acting?

Do you weep at insurance commercials, or are you loath to
show emotion, especially in public?

Are you a whiz at math but can't stand English, or vice versa?

Are you a hugger, or do you prefer to maintain strong physical boundaries with other people?

Do you like classic rock or jazz?

We could go on and on. Fortunately, there is no right answer
to any of these questions. We humans are all wired so differently,
and those unique traits and ways of interacting with the world do
not change when we have suffered a loss. This is another factor
that the stages of grief and other popular theories fail to take into
account. Our current psychological and cultural ideas of grief need
an overhaul, in no small part because they continue to emphasize a
one-size-fits-all approach, even as we recognize the extent to which
our individuality shapes the way we deal with stress and pain.

Beginning with Freud and for decades hence, the dominant
theories about how humans function were "deterministic";

they assumed that we were driven by unconscious dynamics or primitive, animal-like responses to external stimuli. That line of thinking greatly influenced one-size-fits-all grief theorists, from Freud to Kübler-Ross and beyond.

But roughly forty years ago, when I was in training, another way of looking at why we do what we do had found its place in psychological schools of thought. Humanistic theory and therapy emphasized the uniqueness, wholeness, and personal power of each individual. Humanistic therapy focuses on personal experience as a means of determining what a person needs in order to work through his or her problems. The idea seemed to offer the possibility of more flexibility in grief counseling.

Historically, extroverts and emotive people have been seen as the healthy ones. Woe to the quieter individuals who were cautious and shy around other people and who tended to internalize their feelings. In the past, these folks were said to be "repressing." But more and more clinicians are now embracing the notion that differences in personality are—except in extreme cases—totally benign, totally okay. Although the old deterministic school still tends to prevail, it is more and more acceptable to be an introvert, or a person more prone to thinking than overtly feeling. Today hundreds of "type" tests help describe personality without labeling someone as healthy or unhealthy.

Knowing yourself and understanding your unique way of interacting with the world is very important as you seek to reduce the anxiety or shame that comes from feeling that you have to get grief right. Your personality, life experiences, and wiring will dictate, to a significant degree, how you experience loss and what you need from yourself and others as grieving unfolds. You will learn your unique "normal."

Take a few minutes now to set this book aside and close your eyes. After a few deep breaths, focus on your feelings, particularly with regard to your loss. Notice what you feel and, if possible, where in your body your feelings seem to reside. Now think of how you would be most comfortable expressing those feelings. Maybe it's by talking to a friend. Maybe it's by going for a run, or writing in your journal, or listening to music, or screaming into a pillow, or praying, or meditating, or doing yoga, or attending a support group.

Think about how your basic personality type might influence how you grieve. Do you crave interaction with others, or do you prefer to be alone? Is it more important for you to understand or to feel? Do you feel compelled, as many these days do, to read everything you can find about grief? Do you feel the need to express and honor your grief by serving others—volunteering at a children's hospital, food pantry, or nursing home? Some people need to write or to blog. Some need to sit in a special chair. Some need to arrange a photo album. Some need to donate money or become involved in a cause. Some need to ritualize their grief—light the same candle every night or visit the cemetery once a week. All of these can be healthy mourning behaviors according to a person's sense of what they need and who they are.

When you've opened your eyes, it might be helpful to jot down your feelings and thoughts in your journal. And again, know this: *no one else will feel the way you do or will seek to express those feelings in the same way.* Write that sentence down. Claim it. Also know that if you repeat this exercise a year from now, the feelings and ways of expressing them will be different. You are dynamic and changing, and so is your experience of your loss.

In the majority of cases, what people feel or experience as they grieve is normal and healthy, but how they express it might not be. Avoiding behaviors that *don't* serve you is another way to stay connected to your grief. The goal is to stay present to your grief story, as painful as it might be, and to try not to run from it. However you might try to escape, grief will be waiting for you, in one form or another.

As I said in chapter 1, immediately after Ryan's death, I engaged in more than my share of escape behaviors. Even today, I know I tend to overeat and don't get enough sleep when I've suffered a loss. I don't need to gain ten pounds every time someone dies, but it's a big struggle for me to manage my food intake and my sleep when I'm feeling the inevitable pain of grief.

Granted, for a person in the throes of mourning, some numbing out and distraction are necessary. That's why God created crossword puzzles, golf, gardening, coffee shops, and movies (preferably comedies). What are your healthy distractions? The key is to distinguish healthy distractions—activities that allow you to pause your feelings for a moment, so that you are able to come back and be truly present with them later—from activities you are doing to suppress or avoid painful or uncomfortable feelings. And you are the only one who knows the difference.

I try to help my clients achieve a sense of balance. I would never say don't go shopping or have a glass of wine or relax in front of the television. But mindlessly watching seven hours of football or ten straight episodes of *Game of Thrones* might be another story. As is having a third glass of wine or mindlessly maxing out your credit card in a shopping binge.

A client who had recently lost his spouse complained to me that he spent half of his workday lost in thought about his loss or surfing the Internet. He needed to get back to being more productive. So we worked out a program.

"Let's not go for a hundred percent concentration," I said. "What would eighty percent of the day look like?" It looked a lot more productive and satisfying, as it turned out.

I also suggest to clients that for every hour they spend watching TV, they spend a half hour journaling about their loss.

Don't beat yourself up if you have that extra piece of cake or second glass of wine. Just try to turn back to the healthier ways of coping. If the compulsion to act in unhealthy ways gets to be overwhelming, find an "accountability partner." The very act of reaching out to a trusted person often creates the comfort you seek and deflates the desire to act in a self-defeating way.

It's equally important to remember that, just as you deserve to feel and express yourself according to your own desires and personality, those around you have the same need. It is indeed a challenge to honor your own feelings while making room in your heart for the unique coping styles of others, especially those closest to you. The inability to do so has been the source of much added stress for couples and families mourning the same loss.

My clients John and Liz are a good example of how our differences in this area can cause problems. Their marriage had been a long and happy one; as they sat in my office, holding hands, it was clear that they still adored each other. But it was also obvious that they occupied opposite ends of the personality spectrum. John was a successful real estate agent and looked and dressed the part. His charisma filled a room. Liz was pleasant, but very quiet, and chose her words carefully.

They had successfully negotiated their differences over the years. But their ability to do so had broken down after their son had died from complications of HIV. Both were devastated and concerned about the impact of the loss on their other children. But that was not why they sought me out. John and Liz felt increasingly distant from each other—so much so that they worried their marriage was at risk.

Arguments had gotten more frequent. She resented that he was rarely home. When he wasn't working, he channeled his sorrow into volunteer work for HIV-related causes. He loved to tell stories about his son and wept openly when he did. Liz grieved privately and more analytically. She read several books on grief and poured her feelings into a journal, but she was far less outwardly emotional than her husband. That left her vulnerable to his judgment, which she resented. She was also lonely.

He felt he was dealing with his grief more authentically. In fact, John wondered whether Liz was grieving at all. He and his wife had expected to lean on each other after their son's death, but tension and resentment often obscured their sorrow.

"I can't stand the idea of losing her, too," the tearful husband told me in our first session.

"I feel the same way," Liz said.

I was quickly able to broaden their perspective.

"I've heard your story many times before," I said.

"You have?" Liz said.

"This is tricky, and I won't lie to you—a lot of marriages don't survive because of the kinds of issues you're facing now," I said. "But I don't see that here. You are two very different people, but you've made that work. Those differences have been a strength of your marriage, not a weakness. Am I right?"

John smiled.

"Yin and yang," he said.

Liz laughed.

"We still haven't figured out which is which," she said.

"Now you've both suffered a loss so terrible that you assumed it would be different this time," I said. "Yet as hard as this has been, you are both still who you are. That doesn't mean one of you is grieving right, and the other is grieving wrong."

The tension between them evaporated immediately. They were able to connect better in their mutual mourning by remembering and reaccepting their differences. I never saw them again.

The same dynamic plays out again and again for couples who have suffered loss. In the mid-1980s, for my doctoral dissertation, I interviewed ten couples who had recently experienced the loss of a baby to sudden infant death syndrome (SIDS). My research sought to evaluate the impact of such a tragedy on marriage.

I was amazed by the uniformity of what I heard. Every couple I interviewed had reached a crisis point in their relationship because they had either failed to acknowledge or had misinterpreted their partner's unique way of grieving. He thought she didn't need him because she spent so much time talking with friends. She thought he didn't care because he was more withdrawn and showed less emotion. They weren't naming their differences; instead, they were running with their unchecked narratives of what they thought the other was doing.

The remedy was communication.

"I know you need space, but there are times I need to be close to you."

"I know you need to talk to your friends, but I need for you to talk to me, too. Can we find a middle ground so both of us can get our needs met better?"

Of course, the same challenges present themselves whenever people grieve in community. If I see a family of five grieving the death of a mother, I expect five different expressions of mourning, though there is typically some overlap. In such cases, it takes wisdom and compassion to make room for each person to grieve in their own way and to know that there are limits to how family members can support each other when everyone is doubled over from loss.

≋

Several years ago, I was asked to help support members of a neonatal unit at a nearby hospital where the medical team had unexpectedly lost a patient. The nurses and technicians—men and women—were visibly distraught and eager to share their feelings. But as we sat together initially, the doctor who led the team never lifted his eyes from an open textbook. The tension was obvious. Tearful nurses spoke of the death and glanced at the doctor, who sat impassively, looking down. I addressed the tension in the room.

> It's important to explore both the medical reasons for this baby's death and your feelings about it. And all of you need to process what has happened in your own way. Some folks are more emotional and need to talk. With something like this, others need to understand what happened medically. But wherever you are, let's put the medicine aside for now. You all can meet again later to discuss that part of it. But I don't think we can address that and your sadness and upset at the same time.

It was pretty clear to everyone who my comments were addressed to. The doctor closed his book and looked around at his staff.

"You're right. I'm sorry," he said. "We can talk the medicine later."

"Thank you, Doctor," a nurse said. "We know baby Brian's death was hard on you, too."

"It was," he said. "I guess you never get used to it."

The energy in the room shifted with those few words, with the tacit acknowledgment by that nurse that the loss was heartbreaking for the doctor, too, though he might show it differently.

The doctor's behavior, which others felt was insensitive and off-putting, was, in reality, just different. To deal with his pain, the doctor most needed to explore whether a mistake had been made, whether he and his team had done all they could to save their young patient. What he wrestled with was a sense of responsibility and guilt. Other team members needed to examine those things, too, but their priority was to address the feelings of loss that had been brought on by their love for the baby and his family.

The group eventually got to a place of accepting that they were all struggling, just not about the same things at the same time. With that acknowledgment, the team came together. The staff felt safe to speak of their sorrows, or not speak of them, in their own ways.

Notice the subtle but important differences in the terms used to describe loss. *Grief* and *mourning* are often used interchangeably, but they actually speak to different parts of the experience. The definition of *grief* is "sorrow or mental anguish resulting from loss." In other words, it is a noun that describes the feelings.[1] *Mourning* is a verb that describes the act of expressing grief. As leading grief expert Alan Wolfelt put it, "Grief is what we think and feel inside after a loss. Mourning . . . is the expression of our thoughts and feelings outside of ourselves."[2]

So is it possible to grieve and not mourn? To feel sorrow but not express it some way? Shakespeare had an opinion. "Give sorrow words," the bard wrote. "[T]he grief that does not speak / Whispers the o'er-fraught heart and bids it break."[3] But speaking our sorrow is not the only way to mourn. There is also prayer, meditation, listening to music, singing, journaling, and the many other examples cited earlier in this chapter.

You can add any number of your own. I know a woman who rarely spoke of her loss but visited her husband's grave every day. She was certainly mourning.

Is there a wrong way to grieve? That question has been a preoccupation of my profession since Freud. By definition, *pathological grief* means the presence of physical or mental illness or deviation from the normal and healthy. The definition of pathological grief has been remarkably elastic, inconsistent, and flat out wrong in so many instances. I remind you of the newspaper article from chapter 2, in which experts decreed that anyone who has not marched through the stages in six months might need professional help.

I'm trained to diagnose psychological pathology and am always on the alert for signs of it in my grieving clients. It's essential that things like major depression, suicidal thoughts, and panic disorders are diagnosed and get proper attention and treatment. It is my job to recognize those conditions when they exist and to take the necessary steps to keep my clients safe. But sometimes, distinctions between normal grieving and something more serious are blurry. For instance, there has been much debate in recent years about the similarities and differences between clinical depression and the situational sadness of loss.

The deep sorrow of grief and clinical depression *do* share similarities, such as changes in eating and sleeping habits, low energy, and difficulty concentrating and experiencing pleasure. But they differ in important ways. A grieving person will more likely seek to reach out and share the experience and will, at least in the best of circumstances, expect to receive some support. Depression is isolating. In grief, emotions like sadness and anger are magnified; depression numbs our feelings. Grief, as we have seen, can be life and soul affirming; depression is often accompanied by self-loathing and feelings of insignificance.

The stress of grief can indeed morph into depression, especially if a person lacks support or healthy ways to manage stress. All of us go through life with brains that are flawed and imperfect in some way. For example, if you have suffered from chronic depression or anxiety before your loss, those conditions could intensify after one.

I urge you to seek help if you have any doubts about your mental state. Err on the side of caution if you are concerned. As has been the case with so many of my clients, maybe all you need is reassurance that what you are feeling is normal. I know from long experience that this is often the case. We clinicians have historically overdiagnosed pathology relating to grief, to the detriment of patients and clients. Grief is not a medical condition. We professionals should learn how to better care for and support the bereaved and stop treating grief as an illness in such a knee-jerk way.

Embracing your uniqueness, accepting the uniqueness of others who share your loss, coming to terms with frailties and how you deal with stress—all these things will bring measures of peace and will deepen you as a person. Although grief is uninvited, be open to what it will teach you about yourself.

7

HOW DEATH COMES

often sit with clients who struggle to feel the sorrow of their loss—they can't stop thinking about the call in the middle of the night or are preoccupied with the mental image of their loved one's lifeless body in the emergency room.

"You would think that after six months (or nine months or a year), I would have been able to put those things out of my mind," clients will say.

That is when I suggest that they use a little more self-compassion as they allow themselves to reflect on the terrible, traumatizing experience they have endured.

"It's totally understandable to me that the trauma is still following you around. That's the way the brain works," I might say. "That does not mean there is anything wrong with you."

Again, a major goal of this book is to help reduce fear and self-criticism *of your grief.* The sorrow of grief is burden enough. An important part of normalizing the experience of grief is to take into account how your loved one died, as that could have a significant bearing on what you will experience afterward. In other words, the way death comes will probably be an important part of your narrative to explore and embrace.

All death is traumatic at some level. The moment of it brings us face to face with the mystery and finitude of life. It takes us back to the place where we are reminded that we, too, will die. But with death comes a broad spectrum of trauma. The more traumatic the death, the more shocking it is to the brain, and the more likely that the aftereffects of trauma will intrude upon or even monopolize grieving, possibly for a long time. That's a hard reality, perhaps, but there is comfort in knowing that truth.

At one end of the spectrum is the so-called "good death," a peaceful passing at the end of a long life that was well lived. With a good death, terrible suffering was minimal. There was time to resolve any lingering conflicts or hard feelings between the dying person and closest family member and friends. There were chances for important last conversations and goodbyes. The dying person had a say in how their dying went, such as being able to die in an environment familiar to them. There were times to give and receive expressions of love and gratitude.

Although the finality of a good death is inevitably jarring, there tend to be fewer regrets. There is a certain rightness, beauty, and sacredness to it. But that does not necessarily diminish the intensity of the sorrow, particularly if there was a great deal of love and attachment to the one who was lost. (I will talk about this in the next chapter.) However, fewer layers of pain, like remorse, guilt, and blame, are added on top of the grief.

If you were fortunate enough to experience a good death with your loved one, take a few minutes to reflect on it. Feel the pain of your loss, but also notice the grace notes that were probably part of the transition.

- What were the months or weeks like leading up to the death?

- How did your loved one feel or talk about their upcoming death?

- What were the responses of the others who were present in the days before and at the time of death?

- Although the death was anticipated, what, if anything, surprised you about the experience?

For ninety percent of the people I see, something about their loss complicated their sorrow. If I see one sixty-year-old adult child whose mother died a peaceful, pain-free death, I see ten other clients who experienced death in a more traumatic or complicated way. Most often, complicated sorrow happens when death is premature (before reaching the end of the natural life span) or suddenly—or both. I've personally experienced the spectrum of trauma in the three primary deaths I've suffered. And I know firsthand how the different levels of trauma affect grieving.

My mother, DeVere O'Malley, was a remarkable woman of limitless energy who was devoted to her children, her church, and her vast assortment of friends. Though diagnosed with leukemia in her later years, she continued to travel the world with friends much younger and to compete as a runner and cyclist into the last year of her life.

Although her disease finally would have its way, the end of her life was beautiful. On the night before she died, she and I sat on her bed watching TV. We reminisced about our old neighborhood, laughing together at the memories.

She took a turn the next morning.

"I love you, mother," I said when I got to her bedside.

She barely had the strength to reply.

"I love you, too," she said.

I sat on her bed, reading the Psalms. When she took her last breath, Mother was surrounded by her children and grandchildren. Even though her final moments were peaceful, I was heartbroken. It was a shock to have her gone. My mother was someone I had never not known. She was witness to my first breath, and I, to her last—part of the great mystery of life.

But I felt so grateful to be with her at the end. There is no more sacred intimacy than that. Although I still yearn for her, I also feel peace.

Ryan's death was just the opposite. Even though he had been a sick little boy, we had expected him to live. He essentially died in our house. We were witness to it.

My father's death was slightly less traumatic, because he was older. But it was still a shock—it was so sudden, and I had found his body. Also, the last time I had been with him, he had seemed healthy.

Over the years, as I've mourned my son and father, it has been impossible to banish the images of the paramedics who arrived to try to save my son and of my dad sitting in his chair that last time, a book open next to him. Those images are constant companions to my sorrow.

Trauma also often afflicts those whose loved ones died after a long physical decline or disability. A caregiver's exhaustion and worry sap a family's physical and emotional resources, adding another layer of weariness at the time of death and long into their mourning. The primary caregiver can feel emotionally unmoored after months or years of intense focus on the well-being of another. I have seen this in people of all ages, from parents caring for ill or disabled children, to those in midlife caring for spouses or parents, to elderly people who care for a husband or wife to the end.

Elderly people typically come to see me because their adult children believe it will be helpful. That was the case with Peg, who had just lost her husband of sixty-one years. Her daughter, Ruth, sat in on our first session and did much of the talking.

"Dad had Alzheimer's," Ruth said. "We all tried to help take care of him as much as possible, but Mom was the one who was there, all day, all night, for the last six years. I don't know how she did it, but I never heard her complain."

Ruth looked at her mother.

"I'm worried about you, Mom," the daughter said. "All that time you took care of Dad. What do you do now? No wonder you seem depressed lately."

"I'm just tired," Peg replied.

"I think it's more than that," her daughter said.

In our second session, I asked to see Peg alone.

"Would you tell me about your husband?" I said.

Peg paused, as if she weren't prepared for the question. But she began to describe a wonderful marriage, years of caring for her husband through his devastating illness, and the confusion she felt since his death. She said she would not change a thing about their lives together, except for the anguish at the end.

"I read a magazine article the other night that said widows can feel they've lost an arm or a leg," she said. "They generally get along okay, but a part of them is always missing. That's how I feel."

"Of course you do," I said. "It makes perfect sense you would feel that way. It also makes sense you feel so tired. Anyone would be after what you've been through."

I remember how she reached for her purse, pulled out a tissue, and dabbed at her eyes.

"What will I do now?" she said.

"I can't answer that question for you," I said. "But it seems to me that after you rest, you have a lot of life left to live."

In a subsequent session, Peg told me she had begun to volunteer at a local center for Alzheimer's patients. "It gives me a reason to get out of bed in the morning," she told me, chuckling.

If your loved one died after a long illness and you were a caregiver, reflect on these questions as they relate to your story:

- Did you suffer from caregiver fatigue? If so, how did you attempt to manage it?

- Did your loved one suffer terribly? If so, how did that affect you?

- Did you experience any level of trauma or shock when the death occurred?

- Did others assist you in caregiving?

- Was hospice care available to your loved one? Did you find that helpful?

- Did you need time to physically recover after the death of your loved one? Did you get the time you needed?

At the severest end of the spectrum are bereaved clients who suffer from what is known as post-traumatic stress disorder (PTSD), which accounts for about twenty percent of all grieving people who come to me.

Among them was Kara, whose husband, Luke, had gone off to run a mundane errand, buy milk, and put gas in his car. An hour later, two police officers knocked on her door. They told her Luke was dead, caught in the crossfire of a shootout between rival street gangs. Kara insisted that the officers had the wrong address, that there was some horrible mistake. He was just going out for milk.

They described her husband and his car. They handed her his wallet.

"I remember looking at them and seeing their lips move, but it was like my brain had completely shut down," she told me in our first session, two months after her husband's death. "I had no thoughts, no feelings, nothing. I just stood there like a zombie. Then I felt like I was going to faint."

Her living nightmare was just beginning. The horrific way her husband died added layers of mental chaos and suffering on top of Kara's feelings of loss. Because of PTSD, associated thoughts and images overwhelmed and preoccupied her long after her husband's death. Kara, as many who suffer in that way, wondered whether she was losing her grip on sanity.

If the loss you've experienced was sudden or traumatic, your story of grief will almost certainly include emotional pain and mental upheaval beyond sorrow. This does not mean you are crazy or defective; it just means you are grappling with a natural by-product of an experience that will be difficult to sort through alone. I'll describe the symptoms of PTSD in just a bit. But as you explore your story, if you have any doubts about whether you are suffering from PTSD, or if your thoughts or feelings are overwhelming, it's important that you seek professional help. Acute trauma heightens the risk of numerous psychological symptoms.

Trust your own instincts on this score. There is no shame in putting down this book and picking it up again with a therapist.

The diagnosis of PTSD was created in 1980 to describe psychological and physical symptoms that lingered long after a person had endured a traumatic event. At the time, it was most often applied to veterans returning from the war in Viet Nam. In the decades since, however, clinicians have applied it to survivors of car crashes, natural disasters, mass shootings, and child abuse, as well as a number of other intense psychological events.

In PTSD, the fight, flee, or freeze mechanisms—chemical triggers in the brain set off by a traumatic event—do not shut down after the danger has passed. The brain continues to operate as if the threat were still present.

The three most common symptoms are known clinically as hyperarousal, intrusion, and avoidance. Hyperarousal compromises the brain's ability to accurately evaluate danger. Everyday aspects of a person's environment are now seen as threats. An afflicted person startles easily, can have difficulty sleeping, and is often moody and irritable. Another word for intrusions is *flashbacks,* or images from the traumatic event intruding upon awareness with no warning, creating a sudden change in mood or state of mind. Avoidance is the chronic and often unreasonable attempt to steer clear of anything, even the subtlest reminder, of the traumatizing event. Substance abuse and other compulsive behaviors are means of avoidance. Other behaviors include avoidance of funerals, social isolation, and detouring away from a place where a traumatic event occurred.

How do I treat clients suffering from PTSD? First, there is education to let them know that what they are experiencing is neither unnatural nor unexpected. Many are relieved to hear that what they are experiencing is similar to what those who have gone through the horror of war suffer. Clients ask, "Why do these things cause me to melt down?" or "Why are these terrible thoughts playing in a loop in my head?" I tell them, "It's miserable, but this is your brain's attempt to sort through what happened and reorient itself. You are not going crazy."

Clients who have suffered traumatic loss certainly present a more complicated therapeutic challenge, because both trauma issues and the underlying anguish of loss need to be addressed. Clients are often unable to fully touch the pain of their grief until the symptoms of trauma have lessened. And that often doesn't come until after the story of the trauma has been talked through many times in a safe therapeutic environment. The repetition of the story allows the brain to assimilate the images and memories of the traumatic event. With familiarity, the brain's defense mechanisms trigger less and less. Life is no longer one continuous nightmare.

More and more innovative therapies are being developed to help with trauma, and I predict that more will be developed. For example, I often refer my PTSD clients to biofeedback and neurofeedback therapies as an additional support to deal with the complex physiology of traumatic loss. In the past several years, I have also written supportive documents for traumatized clients who have benefited from an emotional support animal.

In the months after Luke's death, Kara could not sleep, lost her appetite, could not concentrate, and had no energy. She was haunted by the notion that her husband's killer had not been caught. She checked four and five times to make sure her doors were locked before she went to bed.

"Every stranger I see could be Luke's killer," she told me. "Everywhere I go, I wonder. Loud noises freak me out. When I do sleep, it is very lightly, and I can barely get up the next morning. I don't even feel like I can grieve for Luke, because my mind is always racing. This is not my usual way to be. I am usually very calm."

Kara and I met regularly for two years. In session after session, Kara talked about the last time she saw her husband, the knock on her door, the shock. Each time that she talked of the horror, it became a little less dreamlike, a little more real. Her brain gradually assimilated what had happened, as terrible as it was.

Nine months after Luke was killed, police arrested a seventeen-year-old boy, a member of a local street gang. Kara felt more secure almost immediately. It wasn't until then that she could actually "be with" her grief for Luke, as she put it. She and I started to talk more about her life with her husband and less about the terrible way it had ended.

The daughter of my clients Jack and Tara was killed when a drunk driver broadsided their car. The parents, who suffered minor injuries, were haunted by the image of their daughter's lifeless body in the backseat as paramedics tried to save her. That image played on an endless loop in their minds, especially when they attempted to sleep. Tara had been driving at the time of the accident and could not get behind the wheel without suffering a panic attack. The couple veered back and forth between intense sorrow of loss and the horrifying mental images.

"It really feels like I'm losing my mind," Jack said. "I see her lying in the car. Then I find myself in Missy's room, remembering her as a little girl and all the wonderful times we had.

One seems like a nightmare; the other, a bittersweet dream. It really does feel like I'm losing my mind."

We met for more than a year, intentionally moving back and forth between the story of the horror and the story of their grief. Helping them understand the complex nature of PTSD alleviated their fear that they were slipping into mental illness. I also taught them to assimilate the trauma symptoms into their lives.

Instead of, "It's crazy that I'm afraid to drive. I've been driving for thirty years," Tara would now say to herself, "No wonder I want to avoid driving. My brain can't forget what happened that night in the car." That repeated self-assurance eventually allowed her to get back behind the wheel. I taught both parents to understand why the images flooded their brains and to accept them when they did. That acceptance helped reduce a layer of stress.

Over time, the intensity of the trauma symptoms began to lessen. More and more of our time together was spent talking about Missy and the profound sorrow they felt at her absence.

If significant trauma was associated with your loss, looking at it directly and repeatedly is the way to reduce its power. You might find the following questions helpful in that regard. Again, set the book aside if you begin to feel overwhelmed. It might be better to think about the questions with the guidance and support of a therapist.

- How did you learn he had died?

- Where were you and what were you doing when you found out?

- Did you witness the death? Was your life threatened?

- How did you get to the emergency room? What did you see, hear, and smell when you arrived?

- Do you have intrusive images from what you witnessed or what you have constructed in your thoughts about the trauma?

In the case of interruptive and traumatic death, mourning is often complicated by another feeling—guilt—which can also be hard to untangle.

As I tell my clients, guilt is not necessarily a bad thing. When we have done something wrong or have hurt people, it is the sign of a healthy conscience. The key is to determine whether guilt is justified or whether a person is being overly responsible.

I often ask my clients to look at it this way: If they put the question before a jury of their peers, what would be the verdict? Yes, they did something for which they should feel guilty? Or, no, they did nothing wrong? Most times, the verdict would be the latter.

Acute guilt has afflicted every client of mine whose loved one died of suicide. Steven and Marissa came to see me shortly after the suicide of their twenty-four-year-old son, Jimmy. The couple had tried to return to their normal routines but remained sleep deprived and tearful.

"Our friends say they hope we can find closure," Steven told me. "But how in the world can a person ever find closure with something like this? Where did we go wrong?"

"That's the question I'll try to help you answer," I said. "We can talk about every part of Jimmy's life. If we find something you should feel guilty about, I promise you, we will face it. But for now, I'd like to get to know Jimmy through your eyes."

They told me the story of a little boy who suffered from developmental problems from the time he went to school and who never seemed to fit in with other children. They were conscientious parents who regularly sought the help of professionals. They sent Jimmy to special camps that might help build social skills. They made sure other kids were welcome in their home. But nothing really seemed to help.

"I've heard lots of stories of parents with challenging children, and you did all you could," I said. "You didn't miss anything. Did you get tired? Did you say some things to Jimmy that you might regret? Of course, but that is part of being a human family."

"I can't tell you how important that is to hear," Marissa said.

The couple eventually started sleeping better and reengaged socially. They joined a support group and eventually became leaders of it, using their experience to help others.

With sudden death, relationships are frozen in time. That is an invitation to another form of guilt that comes with the thoughts of "what if" and "if only."

> "I never took him fishing like I promised.
> If only I had."

> "What if I had kept her at home for another
> five minutes?"

> "I wouldn't have said that if I had known I
> would never see her again."

I've worked with hundreds of clients like Carol, who was haunted with regret because of her last words to her older sister. She is also an example of a person who had something to feel legitimately remorseful about.

Carol's relationship to Rebecca had always been a roller coaster of love, admiration, frustration, and, at times, outright animosity. Carol had always believed that Rebecca was flighty and chaotic, which led to frequent arguments when the two went into business together. Their last conversation came on the telephone, after Rebecca had missed another important deadline.

"You've always felt that the rules didn't apply to you," Carol said. "I've had it. I'm going to find another partner."

Then she hung up. A few hours later, Rebecca suffered a brain aneurysm and died. Carol said she replayed the last conversation over and over with every waking hour, and it kept her up at night.

"My God, it all seems so trivial now," she said. "I mean we had that same argument ten times, and we always figured it out. We would have this time, too."

I encouraged Carol to tell me the whole story of life with Rebecca. The grieving sister came to understand that there was much more to their relationship than the way it ended. But it was also necessary for Carol to own up to the fact that her last words were cruel and that she was overly judgmental about Rebecca's way of being in the world.

I encouraged Carol to journal about her regrets and to write herself a letter of forgiveness. With her regrets addressed head on, she could connect more with her deep sorrow about losing her sister.

What is known as survivor's guilt can be particularly difficult; it often has no basis in logic but can be a powerful emotional response. Why did one soldier step on the land mine and not another? Why did one person survive the attacks of 9/11 when so many others did not? Why did one passenger survive an automobile accident and two did not? Survivor's guilt requires a careful examination of the story behind it. Doing so helps survivors see that, practically speaking, they had no control or responsibility over who died and who didn't.

When I work with people wrestling with these questions, I invariably suggest that some questions just don't have good answers and will remain in their loss story as unanswerable.

My client, a combat veteran named Terry, was standing ten yards away when his best friend, Will, was killed by an explosive device. Terry's severe guilt completely impeded his mourning for his friend.

We carefully talked through the combat death. In doing so, Terry came to accept that his behavior did not contribute in the least to what happened. But then we had to wrestle with more cosmic questions.

"But he was a much better person than me," Terry said. "It's not fair that he's dead and not me."

"I can't say whether Will was a better person or not," I said. "But so many things aren't fair. There really isn't anything we can do but accept that life can seem awfully random and very fragile. What's the reason Will died and you didn't? There isn't one."

Terry gradually came to accept that fact. His feelings of sorrow for the loss of Will increased as his guilt subsided.

If you struggle with survivor's guilt, the following questions might help you explore it and find some acceptance.

- Do you believe there is something you could have done that would have prevented her from dying?

- What medical decision did you make for him that you wish you could change?

- What were your last words with him before the accident?

- What was the level of conflict or peace in your relationship with her?

- Why him and not you?

- What do you need to forgive yourself for in your relationship with her?

Finally, blame is also common in traumatic loss, and it complicates grieving. Richard came to see me because he was "obsessed" with anger toward the truck driver and the trucking company he held responsible for his son's death. The truck driver had been cited several times in the past for speeding and other traffic violations, to the point that his driver's license had been suspended. Yet the trucking company had allowed him to drive anyway.

By any reasonable standard, Richard was justified in his anger. He sued the company, poured a great deal of emotional and physical energy into the court fight, and won a sizable financial settlement. But his anger remained and would only abate with several glasses of Scotch at the end of the day. It was after Richard was arrested for driving while intoxicated that he sought me out.

It was a hard road for him, but I helped Richard experience his anger in its purest form, without the anesthesia of alcohol. As with trauma victims, I assured him that, under the circumstances, his anger was understandable. But I also explained that he had done all he could to make sure the company suffered the consequences. As I would with someone who suffers from survivor's guilt, I suggested that there was no explanation for why his son had been victimized by the trucking company's neglect, as opposed to some other innocent driver. Richard eventually accepted that the only person being harmed by his lingering anger was himself.

If your loss was the result of the action of others, reflect and write about these questions:

- How did you think about the person or persons responsible for her death at the time it occurred?

- Have your thoughts or feelings changed over time?

- Was the person held accountable for his death and did justice occur? If not, how does that feel?

- Have you been able to forgive the person? Do you feel any need to forgive the person?

If your loved one died from any circumstance that created physical or emotional experiences beyond sorrow, that is also part of your grief story. Whether or not you require professional help as you process the multiple layers of thoughts, feelings, or physical responses, be assured that you are not wrong or defective for what you are experiencing.

Before we move on, I want to share this account from my own life. It speaks to many of these dynamics, such as guilt, self-blame, trauma, and remorse. It also speaks to how these emotions can last for decades when the story is withheld because of a family secret about the loss.

Several years ago, on a business trip to the East Coast, I took a detour to my dad's hometown of Scranton, Pennsylvania. I found the cemetery where my grandparents and uncle were buried. Standing there, I suddenly fully understood the enormity of the losses my father had suffered. It was my inherited story of loss.

I had been twenty when I heard the story for the first time. I was home from college, and Nancy and I were engaged. I guess my father felt like he could finally speak to me, man to man. We were standing in the kitchen, and I don't remember how exactly it came up.

"You know my mother committed suicide, right?" he said. "That has haunted me my whole life."

My father had never been so vulnerable with me. He said he was ten when his mother died. His father said the cause was pneumonia, but even as a boy, my dad knew better. He knew his mother had not been sick, but no one would tell him the truth.

What he did not know he attempted to imagine, an example of the need to create stories so that we can try to make sense of our world. But my father was haunted by the story he created: A few months before her death, his mother had tripped on one of his toys and fell, crushing the crystal glass she had been carrying. Her hand was permanently deformed. Dad's story was that his mother had committed suicide because he had left his toy on the floor.

His anguish was obvious as we talked that night. After she died, no one mentioned his mother's name, which was a source of even more guilt for him. He lived in the lie and held himself responsible. That night in the kitchen, I felt deep sadness and compassion for my father.

"I really want you to be happy," I said.

Dad returned to Scranton a few years after that conversation and found the doctor who had falsely certified his mother's cause of death. My father's father, who had been a physician, had asked his colleague to cover up the cause.

"I've got one question for you," Dad said. "How did my mother die?"

"She committed suicide," the doctor said. "We should have told you boys. I have carried that with me ever since."

My dad also learned that her death had nothing to do with the toy on the floor. Just that quickly, he had the truth and an apology from a member of the conspiracy of silence. My dad also found a measure of understanding. At the time of his mother's death, suicide was considered a mortal sin in the Catholic Church. She could not have received the rites of the Church, nor could she have been buried in the Catholic cemetery. My dad's father had chosen secrecy over public shame.

When he came home from that trip, my dad seemed like a different man. A weight that he had carried since he was ten years old was finally gone. He had lived with guilt and confusion for a lifetime because of the secret that was kept and the story that was never told. Once he knew the true story, he could step out from the shadow where he had lived and be more present to his life.

8

ATTACHMENT AND GRIEF

For my money, the movie *Cast Away* is one of Hollywood's great love stories—the tale of a deep and abiding bond between a man and his . . . volleyball.

In the popular film from 2000, Tom Hanks played Chuck, a FedEx problem solver whose business flight over the Pacific was caught in a violent storm and crashed. Chuck somehow survived and washed up on a deserted island that would be his solitary home for four years. His only companion was Wilson, the Wilson volleyball that Chuck discovered in a package from the doomed plane that also had washed ashore. The marooned man painted a face on the ball with his own blood. Day after day, Chuck poured out his sadness, loneliness, fear, and frustration to the ball. The stranded man talked over every major event and decision. Wilson and Chuck even quarreled and reconciled. When the time came, Chuck took Wilson onto the makeshift raft that was to be his means of rescue. But early in the voyage, Wilson toppled into the water and was pulled away by the currents. Chuck futilely swam after his companion, nearly drowning himself in the process. He could not have been more devastated if a human companion had floated away.

"Willllllsssssssonnnnnnn!"

One of the first things Chuck did after his rescue and return to civilization was to buy another volleyball.

With Chuck and Wilson, the screenwriters tapped into this basic truth of human existence: we crave attachment. Early in our lives, there is a survival imperative for this attachment. Babies instinctively attach to their parents and caregivers because they are incapable of surviving on their own. Later in life, the desire to attach might be somewhat less primal, but the deep desire remains. Relationships define human experience.

But those human bonds always come with a price. Chuck realized this as Wilson floated beyond his reach. As I've said, I knew the moment my son was born, given his precarious state, that there was a great risk in loving him. My life since Ryan's death is another example of the fact that when we love someone, when we are attached to them, it is our fate to experience mourning and sadness when the attachment is severed by death. That unique relationship is the foundation of our equally unique story about the person who has died. Grieving is another expression of love. As the blogger Tim Lawrence so beautifully put it, "Grief really is love, weeping."[1]

Grieving clients frequently talk about this dilemma after their heart has been broken by loss. "Why should I continue to love when doing so leads to such great pain?" There is no magic answer to this question. To love is to risk pain. But the alternative is to live in loneliness and isolation.

The story of our grief does not begin with death; it begins with the story of life, of love, of attachment. To me, the single biggest reason mourning is unique to every person is that no story of attachment is the same.

Attachment has been a focus of researchers and practitioners in my field going back to Freud. However, this focus is mostly with regard to the psychological development of children. Psychiatrist and psychologist John Bowlby was the pioneer in this regard. Bowlby and his associates made the connection between attachment and grief by studying the reaction of infants and children when their attachment to primary caregivers or other emotional providers was severed through separation or death.[2] Bowlby eventually expanded his research into adult attachment and separation.

As has been the case for many psychological theories through the years, neuroscience has affirmed the power of attachment. Not only is the baby's brain designed to form an attachment to his or her caretakers, but the neural pathways of caretakers are also altered in ways that promote attachment and nurturing.[3] For example, research has shown that the sound of a baby crying causes neurons to fire in certain areas of a mother's brain. We can now describe how attachment happens with the understanding of the part of our brain known as mirroring neurons. "Infants are hardwired to connect with their caretakers," John Prendergast wrote in *In Touch: How to Tune In to the Inner Guidance of Your Body and Trust Yourself*. "They are able to distinguish their mother's face and voice within thirty-six hours of birth."[4]

The foundation of emotional health and security begins when an infant's caregiver mirrors the child's expressions and moods in a safe, loving, and accurate way. According to Prendergast, "When normally responsive mothers face their one-year-old babies without showing any emotion on their faces, babies start to have an emotional meltdown within a minute as their attempts to elicit a response meet with failure."[5]

But you don't need a PhD to understand a basic reality of life. Whether the approach is psychoanalytic, evolutional, or neurobiological, all agree—attachment is essential to survival at the beginning of life and essential to well-being later on.

Reflect on *your* relationship with the one you have lost. The questions that follow are merely jumping-off points to spur your own memories and thoughts of your attachment to the one you lost. I invite you to jot down thoughts, feelings, and memories as they occur.

- What did that person mean to you?

- Who were you with that person that you couldn't be with anyone else?

- How would your life have been different had you never known her?

- What was his personality like?

- What did she look like?

- When was he the happiest?

- How did he make you feel emotionally safe?

- What was your biggest regret?

- What were some of your most meaningful conversations with her?

- What did you most enjoy doing together?

- How did she demonstrate her attachment to you?

- What do you know about his life before he met you?

- What losses did he have?

- What did you most enjoy doing together?

- What values did you share?

- What is the favorite story you like to tell others about her?

- What were his "demons"?

- What was the most surprising thing about him?

- Was your life with him worth the pain you are feeling now?

Add your own questions, unique to your experience.

Your answers to questions such as these will go far to explain your experience of grief. Many times, other people just won't get it. And that is what is known as disenfranchised grief—when the community doesn't support the intensity of a person's grief because of societal notions that such grief is not really warranted.[6]

My client Mark was a young man who felt defective because of the deep sorrow he continued to feel about the death of his grandfather a year before. Mark's friends and family wondered, in so many words, "What's the big deal?" Mark wondered the same thing.

In our culture, there is an unspoken hierarchy of grieving—another example of our need to categorize grief. A parent's loss of a young child is the most painful of all, so parents are seen as the most entitled to grieve. The loss of a sibling is more painful than the loss of a friend. The loss of a parent is more painful than the loss of a grandparent.

Mark's grandfather had lived a long and happy life; his was an example of a "good death." Yet when he came to see me, Mark still found himself tearing up at virtually any reminder of his granddad. Understandably, he felt like he could not confide in anyone else.

"I can't seem to get over it," he said. "That just seems weird."

Then I asked Mark to tell me about his grandfather.

"My parents split up when I was a baby. I remember all those visitation weekends when my mom would have my bag packed and sitting by the door, but my dad never showed. She would then take my bag and unpack it. But I think I was relieved, because my dad was drunk so often, and I never felt safe with him. The one time my dad came to my soccer game, I could hear him screaming at me and screaming at the ref. It was really embarrassing. But I got over it. It didn't seem to matter . . ."

"Because your grandfather was there for you?" I guessed.

"Every game. Didn't matter how I played. 'You gave it your best shot,' he would say. I was with him pretty much every weekend, hunting or fishing. He brought me to his office and to job sites. I was always so proud, and he seemed proud of me. One time, when I was a teenager, I asked him how he had been so successful in life. He just smiled and said, 'Hard work and telling the truth.' I've never forgotten that."

"Your grief would be significant if you were just grieving for your grandfather," I said. "He was a remarkable man, and you never knew life without him. But you are also grieving for the father he was to you; he helped you form into the person you are today. You lost a grandfather and a father."

Mark's story demonstrates how, in so many cases of grief, attachment trumps all. He mattered to his grandfather in ways that he didn't to his father. Once he fully understood his attachment to his grandfather, Mark was able to embrace his sorrow in a way that it deserved. He could also share that knowledge with his family and friends, as a way of explaining why he continued to struggle. Gone was the shame. Mark even felt a certain level of pride in his sorrow, as it reminded him how deeply he loved and had been loved.

Attachment certainly isn't limited to human relationships. Anne's story, another example of disenfranchised grief, is one I hear frequently.

She came to see me after a painful divorce. In her mind, the pain of the breakup was legitimate. She was a deeply introverted person who had few close friends, and no one with whom she felt comfortable sharing her sense of isolation and loneliness. But for most of our first session, she talked about Smokey, her ailing cat.

"She's been with me longer than any human—going on twenty years," she said. "Jobs and people have come and gone, but Smokey has always been there. She doesn't care if I've had a good day or a bad day. I feed her when I get home, and she curls up in my lap no matter what. It might sound weird, but I talk to her."

"If that's the case, I'm weird, too," I said. "I talk to my dog all the time."

Tears welled in her eyes.

"But the vet says he doesn't know how much longer he can keep her going. I don't know what I will do without her."

"I understand," I said.

She seemed surprised by that and relieved.

When Anne arrived for her session a few months later, she broke into tears the moment she sat down.

"I had to put Smokey down," she said. "I called in sick at work. I just couldn't face people. But no one would understand. The girl next to me at work just lost her mother. My cat died."

I assured Anne that her grief was just as valid.

"After twenty years of unconditional love and friendship, you absolutely get to mourn Smokey's death," I said. "Your coworker grieves for her mother for the same reason you grieve for Smokey—a deep attachment. Pet love is as close to unconditional love as we can get. You get to grieve."

"Even it was a cat?"

"Even if it was a cat," I said.

Looking more deeply into Anne's love for Smokey provides a window into the power of attachment more generally. Anne had been hurt in her divorce, but she didn't have any human to share that with at the end of the day. Her reliance on Smokey was tantamount to Chuck's reliance on Wilson the volleyball in *Cast Away*. Anne had formed a ritual with Smokey that was unconditional and predictable. Come home, greet, feed, sit on the couch, talk, watch TV, and feel Smokey purr at her human touch. It was a healthy emotional feedback loop.

Most people who come to me about the loss of a pet are almost always embarrassed; they seek me out because they feel there is no other place to turn. Yet I tell them that pets can provide one of the purest forms of attachment we know, because it is unconditional attachment, without conflict. That is rarely true with another human. Smokey the cat soothed Anne's loneliness and anxiety every night. What human would have been that dependable? No wonder Anne felt bereaved every time she came home and Smokey wasn't there to greet her.

What most people do, and what Anne eventually did, was get a new pet. She mourned, but she also realized she did not have to remain alone. Another cat started to fill that hole in her life again. But Anne would be forever grateful to Smokey, because he was there in the transition. Smokey was the steady, living being after the divorce.

The role of attachment in grief can also be understood by its opposite—a lack of normal attachment. This is an important topic, though one I've seen very little written about.

Over the years, many clients come to me because they are confused that they do not feel more grief or that they are even relieved after the death of a loved one. Cases like this make up a small percentage of my practice, and they are almost certainly underreported because people are embarrassed by their feelings. Relief at the death of another sounds horrible.

There is indeed no Hallmark card of condolence that speaks to this subject. I have never heard a client discuss the feelings of relief, release, or emancipation regarding the death of a person close to them without confusion, shame, apology, or guilt. That's understandable when you consider the ancient imperative of attaching to those in our tribe, particularly those initially responsible for our survival. When the ones who are supposed to be the safest for us are not, the natural order is disrupted.

This issue is known as complicated attachment, which exists on a long continuum. As I've said, every attachment story is unique, and rarely is attachment not complicated by the messiness of human relationships. Recall the story of Carol and Rebecca, the sisters from chapter 7. The two were frequently at odds, and their relationship ended on a very unfortunate note. But after Carol was able to work through her guilt, her deep attachment and love for her sister, as well as her grief, came to the surface.

But it's different when the deceased had perpetrated overt physical or psychological abuse. The resulting relationships are devoid of love and attachment, even though they typically include family. Short of criminal abuse discovered by authorities, these relationships can be almost impossible to escape. A child is attached by blood to an abusive parent, but is not connected in the other, more life-affirming ways. Yet children don't have the option to divorce their parents.

That feeling of there being no escape often leads to post-loss feelings of relief, guilt, anger, and confusion instead of sorrow. Another word that also comes up is *emancipation*. With death, those left behind are free of the oppression of an emotionally or physically unsafe relationship. But without help, it's hard for a person in that situation to know what to do with feelings of emancipation, especially when the world says you are supposed to be sad.

Margaret came to see me six months after the sudden death of her mother. Her mother was a socially prominent woman, and the large church was full for her funeral. The family was inundated with flowers, sympathy cards, and memorials. In our first session, I offered my condolences to Margaret, who shot me an icy look.

"You assume I am sad," she said. "The truth is that I'm relieved. What a horrible thing to say. That's why I'm here. I feel so guilty.

How could any decent person not feel terribly sad after their mother died?"

"Why do you think you feel relieved?"

Margaret hesitated. I could see she was trying to decide whether to spill some family secrets.

"With my mother, it was always about appearances—the right clothes, the right house, the right friends, the right clubs, the right charities," Margaret began. "She constantly shamed and criticized me. I could never get it right for her. I could not have cared less about any of that. She wanted me dressed every day like a child model, and I just wanted to play outside with the other kids. And I was always too heavy. And my hair was always too curly. I always felt like I was supposed to be the right accessory for her, like a piece of jewelry. Thank God for my nanny. She loved me for who I was. I don't know how I would have turned out if she were not in my life."

In high school, Margaret became interested in social justice. She decided to major in social work in college.

"You should have seen my mother's face when I told her. 'You're going to do what?!'" she said. "I guess, after everything, she thought I would marry a rich young man from the country club and take over her role in society. She said she had a 'conflict' and did not come to my college graduation. Never once did she ask me about my work. I haven't regretted my decision, not for a second. But it's easier now that she's gone."

Her relief at her mother's death is perfectly understandable. More than that, Margaret could have felt no other way. Relief came because the struggle to resist her mother's control was finally over.

We dealt with Margaret's guilt at her relief in just a couple of sessions. Her real challenge, as is often the case with complicated attachment, was to come to terms with a different loss—the loss of never having a nurturing mother. A series of letter-writing exercises helped Margaret touch the feelings of loss for what she did not have.

Review the following questions to connect with the story of conflict in grief if that has been your experience. Feeling relief is not a betrayal to the one who died; rather, it is part of your unique story.

- What was the most difficult time you shared?

- What was the biggest source of conflict between the two of you?

- Did you try to resolve the conflict? If so, what happened?

- Were there times when you felt emotionally unsafe with him?

- If able, what do you need to forgive him for?

- What do you need to forgive yourself for in the relationship with her?

However you answer these questions, rest in the knowledge that the pain of complicated attachment and the feeling of relief that comes after death are both parts of your own, unique story of loss.

9

YOUR STORY

Hopefully you have begun to appreciate the importance, power, and uniqueness of your narrative of loss and have come to understand it in much deeper ways. For example, until now, you might not have recognized the role that environmental triggers have played in your grief. They are unavoidable and are to be acknowledged and accepted. You may not have understood the degree to which your personality—your unique way of being in the world—plays into your way of grieving. You may not have allowed for the circumstances of your loss and their impact on you now. You may have a much deeper understanding of how attachment and love—or the lack thereof—affect bereavement.

These are all aspects of your story. Finding your story is the alternative to analyzing your grief and attempting to gauge its "correctness." My mission to this point has been to help you explore your story in all of its beauty, pain, and complexity. Embrace your narrative for what it is—a tale that is unique in human history. Too rarely do we humans fully appreciate the miraculous nature of our lives.

How you approach what comes next in the writing of your story is entirely up to you. In this chapter, I offer ideas and suggestions.

I typically encourage my clients to view their story in three chapters. The first concerns their story of attachment to the one they lost. In the second chapter, we talk about the circumstances of death and the immediate aftermath, such as the visitation, funeral, or other mourning rituals. In our sessions, I ask my clients to talk me through these first two chapters. As I listen, I try to guide their exploration with questions like the ones I have asked you in previous chapters—particularly, in chapters 5–8. Many clients take notes as we speak, wanting to capture memories and feelings as they arise. Clients also journal between sessions and share new insights in my office.

The third chapter is life after loss—that is, the life that is unfolding when clients walk through my door and the one unfolding for you now. This third chapter will go on for the rest of our lives. I encourage my clients, as I encourage you, to keep a grief journal going forward.

You, by necessity, must approach this third chapter differently than my clients. Let me suggest that you write your whole story—all three chapters—in your journal or on your computer. You can use the questions from the book to spur your memories and feelings.

This task can seem daunting, especially if you have never written or kept a journal before. Remember that this writing is just for you. You have all the power. You are discovering your story of grief and should feel free to remember and express yourself as if no one else will ever read what you have written. It's not important that you create a decent piece of writing—or even a coherent one. After all, if you were sitting with me in my office, I would not ask you to structure your words in any particular way. My clients share and express themselves, uncensored and unfiltered. The goal is to approximate, as closely as possible, what you would tell me if you were sitting in my office.

But I do strongly encourage you to write. By doing so, and using the questions and prompts in this book, you will make the feelings and memories that have been floating around inside of you less illusory. Those feelings tend to come and go, but by writing them, you capture them for always. The study guide in this book offers further guidance on writing your story.

Through the act of writing, you are also certain to remember and feel things you would not have otherwise. Keep in mind the words of Dr. Rita Charon: "What comes to pen is not always what comes even to mind."

You've already done much of the hard work in previous chapters by journaling and answering questions. You've gone deep into the details of your story and your relationship with the one you lost. Think back over what you've read and what you've noted in your journal. If certain passages or questions caused you to put down the book and just remember or feel, you might want to start your narrative there.

There is no requirement for length. Your writing can be as long or short as you want to make it. It does not have to come together in a linear way. There will be plenty of time to massage and edit later, if that is your wish.

A few more suggestions: As you explore the first chapter of your story, consider rereading chapter 8 and the questions about attachment found there. Stumped at where to start? Start at the beginning, with the day you met or the day your child was born. From there, describe your relationship with the one you lost chronologically, as if you were telling the story to someone who had never heard it before.

Depending on the depth and length of attachment, scores of memories could be waiting to be retrieved. They reside in your brain, ready to be accessed and decoded. One memory will lead naturally to another as you write. Try to remember as much as you can—and keep remembering. Feelings are likely to come, many of them painful. Let them come and go, without self-judgment.

Now recall your inventory of environmental triggers from chapter 5. The sights, sounds, and smells all contain memories and feelings. These triggers will also help you further recall details of your relationship and the degree of your attachment. Again, you will probably think of things that had never consciously occurred to you. As you reflect on your attachment and the triggers in your environment, you might come to know the person you lost in a deeper way. If this adds to your sadness, that's okay. But it might also deepen your love.

A word to those who felt emancipated by the death of a relative or friend: Focus on the fact that your wish was not that another person die. Rather, it was that the oppression or abuse would end, and it never did. If the relationship was one of being fearful, belittled, minimized, ignored, neglected, abused, abandoned, or engulfed, how could you not feel relief when that has come to an end?

In your story, write the truth of your relationship with the deceased. You are not being disloyal to that person; you are being true to yourself. It might also be helpful to write about the relationship you wish you had had with the person who died. Among other things, it will help you see the gap between what was and what you had hoped for. Include in your story your feelings of grief for what you didn't have.

≈

Now remember the circumstances of death and the days immediately after. (If your memories or feelings become over-whelming, reach out to a professional.) I encourage you to look back at chapter 7 and any questions that might have resonated with your experience. Here are a few more:

- Was the death sudden or violent, or did it occur peacefully at the end of a long, well-lived life?

- Did you find the body? What was that like?

- Were you in the accident?

- Did the telephone ring in the middle of the night? Who called, and what exactly did he or she say?

- When did you last see him?

- What was the last thing she said to you?

- Do you dwell on things like:
  › "If he had stayed five minutes longer or turned left instead of right, he would still be alive."
  › "I wouldn't have said that had I known I would never see him again."
  › "We were supposed to go the ballgame together."

In the case of sudden death, that event is when your story changes forever. The memories of these horrible moments can run in a grieving person's mind on an endless loop. Has that been the case for you? Maybe the loop went on for weeks or months. Maybe it still runs.

If your loved one suffered a traumatic death, it's important to understand that your basic sorrow has a companion, which is the trauma itself. The trauma is part of your story; the more you know about it and the more times you can look at it squarely, the better. In your story, you're writing about the death and how your mind and body reacted to it.

Bear in mind that your responses to the trauma may fall into clinical categories. Explore in your story the extent to which trauma might have included avoidance, hyperarousal, or intrusive thoughts or flashbacks. Don't try to fit your story into these symptoms, but do look at them to see if they are part of your experience.

You may want to work with a professional therapist as you work through this exercise, or you may choose to do it alone. In either case, this exercise (or a version of it) is important. Keep in mind that these experiences are already happening in your life; you're not creating them by writing about them. There is no harm in writing down what you are feeling today.

"I had a flashback that caused me to lose focus at work."

"I drove five miles out of my way to avoid being anywhere close to the scene of the accident."

"I jumped at the sound of a slamming door."

Now let's turn to the days immediately after it happened, including the visitation and the funeral.

- See the faces and hear the voices of those who came to support you.

- Remember how you felt when there were fewer people at the funeral service than you expected.

- What was it like to have a house full of people after the service?

- Did you have exhaustion from the time of caregiving before the death?

- When did you feel most comforted?

- When did you feel most angry, confused, alone, bereft?

- What was it like as you walked from the gravesite?

What if your loss was a "good death"? Although I see fewer clients in cases such as these, profound emotions still accompany any passing. And as I've said, it is impossible to fully prepare for the finality. Explore this idea as you write your second chapter; explain how you thought you had been prepared but felt a great void nonetheless. Be on the lookout for moments of profound love, kindness, and grace.

My coauthor, Tim Madigan, found many of these grace notes in the story of his younger brother, Steve, who died of lung cancer in the summer of 2000. Tim recorded it in his memoir, *I'm Proud of You: My Friendship with Fred Rogers.* By choosing to write about it, Tim captured memories and feelings he would not have remembered otherwise. In doing so, he created a beautiful record of those sacred moments for generations of his family to come, as well as for thousands of readers.

That Thursday morning, I woke up at 6:30 a.m. to take my shift at his bedside, sitting in the living room with my brother-in-law, Jay, and my brother, Mike. At 7:50 that morning, Jay and I were talking about fishing when I saw Steve stir, open his eyes, and rise up out of his bed, lifting both arms toward the ceiling like he had just scored a goal in hockey. Then Steve slumped back down, and by the time I got to his bed, my brother's breathing had changed dramatically, becoming shallower and shallower. Within seconds, each member of our family had surrounded the bed. Steve's wife Cally wept at his side. His sons, Timmy and Tyler, looked frightened and confused at the foot of the bed. My mother held a rosary, praying and crying. My father's face crinkled with emotion. I held Steve's hand and rubbed his forehead, and told him to go be with the angels. Then his breathing stopped.

For nearly two years, ever since Steve was diagnosed, I had thought about that moment, wondering what it would be like. But nothing had prepared me for what I felt as my brother died that morning. In an instant, it seemed as if all the oxygen had been sucked out of the room, replaced by an absence more profound than any I had felt before. The same long body was still lying in the hospital bed, but the unseen thing that had made my brother who he was had gone, had vanished in a mysterious instant. What was that invisible presence that had been the essence of my brother? Where did it go on that sunny August morning? Where is it now? They are questions that I will ask as long as I am alive myself.

Someone shut off the oxygen machine, and there was an eerie stillness in the house. The family lingered by Steve's body for many minutes, kissing him and saying goodbye, then most left the living room and sat together weeping in the bright sunshine of the back porch. My father and I stayed behind in the living room as the funeral home attendants loaded my brother's body into a black bag. Dad and I walked next to the gurney as the attendants carried Steve's body to the white van parked in the driveway. Then I joined the others out back.

"My heart's broke," I told my mother.

"I know," she said.

For the first time that morning, I began to sob.[1]

My first telephone call that morning was to my wife. My second was to the office of Fred Rogers.

"Oh, Tim," he said. "I'm so sorry. I had no idea it was coming so soon."

I have no real clue how we spent the rest of that day, probably moving about in a shocked and grieving stupor. I do know that it was the night of Steve's death that Fred's email message arrived in Steve's computer, was printed, and passed from hand to hand inside my brother's house. The subject line read: "Dear Tim."

"After a long day at work I came home and told Joanne [Fred's wife] about Steve. We talked about you all during dinner. Joanne sends her love to you, too. As usual I went for my after dinner walk in the park near our apartment. It was near sunset . . . and a gorgeous one it was. On my way back home there was the most beautiful cloud formation illuminated by the last bit of setting sun. Tim, there are no words for such beauty. At any rate all I could think to say was 'Thank you,' so I did and prayed for you and your wonderful family gathered in such common purpose there in Iowa. It wasn't long before something said to me, 'Look up.' Well I did and there in a completely clear patch of sky was the brightest new moon I had ever seen. It looked like a special apostrophe in the sky and I thought, 'Yep, it's Steve's for sure.'

"Just wanted you to know that you're all in our hearts more than ever. I'm Proud of You, as always. Fred."[2]

≈

We are living in the third chapter of our grief stories. Typically, in the normal narrative arc of a novel or a movie, this is when resolution comes. But remember this: Our final chapter will have a different ending than a typical book or movie. Although this chapter has a beginning, it really has no ending—or it doesn't end until we do. The third chapter is dynamic. It will change over time, but it will not end.

That might be a troubling notion for many, especially those looking to cross the finish line of mourning, to achieve acceptance or closure. But those things don't actually exist in reality. And would we really want them to? What we're after is to live our grief story going forward, to embrace it and the feelings that are associated with it. We grieve because we love. And the feelings of grief and love that we experience will come up in different contexts as our lives change.

In my case, as our grandchildren are born, I feel more intense yearning for my mother and father, as well as Nancy's parents. I also feel a deep sense of sorrow that they are no longer alive to see the next generation. Every time I try to picture Ryan as a man of thirty-six, I feel a tug of sadness, and that never stops. I wish with all my heart that my second chapter with my son had not happened. But I am in chapter three. I have not finished my story. I carry it with me.

As you explore chapter three of your grief narrative, write about events, thoughts, feelings, and memories from the time of the funeral to now.

- Have you had periods of insomnia?

- Who surprised you with their comfort? Who disappointed you?

- Did your loss affect your religious beliefs or faith?

- Did it affect your close relationships?

- Did you save his last voicemail message? Did you listen to it? How often? What did you feel when you did?

- Could you give away her clothes?

- What was it like to live in the house without her?

- Did you try to avoid your favorite restaurants or parks? Did you consciously return to them? If so, why?

- How was your first major holiday without her?

- What did you do on his birthday?

- Was the second year as painful as the first?

- Have you kept reminders like photographs, plaques, or other sentimental possessions of your loved one in a prominent spot in your home?

By the time you picked up this book, weeks, months, or even years may have passed since your loss. The longer it's been, the more memories of your post-loss life are waiting to be retrieved. Take your time. Approach this part of your story as a kindly objective observer, one who looks on without judgment.

Finally, your grief narrative is about what is happening today and in the months and years to come. Claim that part of your story. As with other parts of the journey, journaling may be useful.

"I had a hard time waking up today."

"I was so annoyed by the person who kept bragging about her child."

"I was so comforted when my coworker put her hand on my shoulder."

"It's opening day. He loved baseball."

"I laughed today when I remembered our first date."

"Hours can pass when I don't think of her at all. Why do I feel guilty about that?"

"The cherry blossoms are out. She always loved those."

"I have never spent a Fourth of July without him."

"I forgot he was gone and picked up the phone to call him."

"I was driving behind the same model of her car tonight."

"I am going to make the scrambled eggs the way she liked them."

"I thought my heart would break when I saw her son walk across the graduation stage."

"How could I miss him this much after all this time?"

So chapter three will go on. Pay attention to its twists and turns, ups and downs. Continue to honor your remarkable story. But for now, congratulations are in order. You've bravely remembered. You've put expectations and self-judgment aside and felt love, joy, resentment, sadness, anger, confusion, gratitude, and regret over this story, which is like no other.

You've done it.

10

THE CULTURE OF POSITIVITY

Now that you've created and embraced your own unique story of grief, it's important to talk about the state of things for the bereaved in our society and in culture more generally. I want you to know that you haven't been imagining things—it is very hard for grieving people out there.

For a series of articles in *Slate* magazine, Meghan O'Rourke and psychologist Leeat Granek surveyed eight thousand bereaved people, focusing on the emotional challenges of those who mourn:

> The most surprising aspect of the results is how basic the expressed needs were, and yet how profoundly unmet many of these needs went. Asked what would have helped them with their grief, the survey-takers talked again and again about *acknowledgment* of their grief. They wanted recognition of their loss and its uniqueness; they wanted help with practical matters; they wanted active emotional support. What they didn't want was to be offered false comfort in the form of empty platitudes.[1]

There is a very good chance that you have felt unsupported in your grief, at least at some level. You may have been bombarded by often hurtful and meaningless clichés from well-intentioned people. Or maybe you felt abandoned by those who are uncomfortable in the presence of human suffering. Fred Rogers also spoke to this sad reality: "People have said 'Don't cry' to other people for years and years, and all it has ever meant is 'I'm too uncomfortable when you show your feelings: Don't cry.' I'd rather have them say, 'Go ahead and cry. I'm here to be with you.'"[2]

See if you can relate to the words of C. S. Lewis, the great writer and theologian who lost his wife to cancer and wrote about his mourning in the classic book *A Grief Observed*:

> An odd by-product of my loss is that I'm aware of being an embarrassment to everyone I meet. At work, at the club, in the street, I see people, as they approach me, trying to make up their minds whether they'll "say something about it" or not . . . I like best the well brought-up young men, almost boys, who walk up to me as if I were a dentist, turn very red, get it over, and then edge away to the bar as quickly as they decently can. Perhaps the bereaved ought to be isolated in a special settlement like lepers.[3]

≋

How did suffering become shameful? I believe a main culprit is our "culture of positivity." Psychologist Stephen L. Salter defined this culture as "the widespread social practice of eliminating any attitude and utterance that doesn't have an uplifting effect on one's mood and those around them." He continued:

The pressure to think positive pervades our everyday language and practices. It's the reflexive response, "Put on a happy face," if we are not smiling. "Think cheerful thoughts and good things will happen." We feel pressure to display a pleasant countenance even if it is insincere. And we often feel guilty if we're not quite able to don that cloak. The underlying belief, it seems, is that hurt and discontent can be done away with simply by acting as though it isn't there.[4]

Author Barbara Ehrenreich also skewered the positivity culture in *Bright-Sided: How the Relentless Promotion of Positive Thinking Has Undermined America*:

> I do not write this in a spirit of sourness or personal disappointment of any kind, nor do I have any romantic attachment to suffering as a source of insight or virtue. On the contrary, I would like to see more smiles, more laughter, more hugs, more happiness and, better yet, joy . . . But we cannot levitate ourselves into that blessed condition by wishing it. We need to brace ourselves for a struggle against terrifying obstacles, both of our own making and imposed by the natural world. And the first step is to recover from our mass delusion that is positive thinking.[5]

Ehrenreich, who ran afoul of the positivity movement when she openly expressed her anger as a breast cancer patient, called the culture an "an obligation imposed on all American adults . . . To the positive thinker emotions remain suspect and one's inner life must be subject to relentless monitoring."[6] Ehrenreich traced the movement to the mid-1800s, when positive thinking was promoted as a healing technique. A century later, Norman Vincent Peale became a cultural icon, and his book *The Power of Positive Thinking* was another gospel of good living.

The sunny theology of television preacher and author Joel Osteen is one more contemporary example. Osteen inspired an Internet firestorm when, in a recent book, he criticized parents who continued to mourn years after the death of their young son:

> Fifteen years after the fact, Phil and Judy continued to languish in self-pity and self-induced isolation. Why? Because they don't want to get well . . . They like the attention too much . . . You must get beyond it. Unless you let go of the old, God will not bring the new. It is natural to feel sorrow and to grieve, but you shouldn't still be grieving five or ten years later.[7]

Grief expert Joanne Cacciatore responded to Osteen:

> Allowing mourners to be in their pain, without trying to make them change how they feel (often to make yourself and said others feel better), would actually be a more compassionate and Christ-like response. Why? Because trying to force a grieving person to feel better is like telling a double amputee to get up and run before she is ready: it's insensitive, lacks circumspection, and certainly doesn't even remotely resemble compassion.[8]

As Ehrenreich concluded, the positive thinking movement encourages intense self-scrutiny of a person's thoughts and judges them against the rubric of optimism and happiness. Negative thoughts are to be avoided, purged, and certainly not spoken of.

The result is to drive crucial parts of our humanity—our true feelings and emotional pain—underground. Happiness, hope, and optimism became positives. Sadness, anger, loneliness, depression, and fear became negatives; they signify weakness or, worse, mental illness.

According to psychotherapist Francis Weller:

> This "psychological moralism" places enormous pressure on us to always be improving, feeling good, and rising above our problems. Happiness has become the new mecca, and anything short of that often leaves us feeling that we have done something wrong or failed to live up to the acknowledged standard. This forces sorrow, pain, fear, weakness, and vulnerability into the underworld, where they fester and mutate into contorted expressions of themselves, often coated in a mantle of shame.[9]

I believe that the positivity movement also has had much to do with our grief- and death-phobic culture. It's exceedingly difficult to put a universally positive spin on death and what grief requires of us, which is openness to our sadness, pain, and confusion. The culture of positivity and resolution theories like the stages of grief seem to go hand in hand. According to them, the quicker you can achieve closure/resolution/acceptance, the quicker you can return to the pre-loss state of sunniness.

The culture of positivity is also reflected in how our funeral practices have changed over the past generation. One aspect is the tendency to put more and more distance between the bereaved and the actual body of the deceased, with more cremation and closed caskets. At the same time, there has been greater and greater emphasis on looking at the bright side. This is not necessarily a good thing. As Thomas Long and Thomas Lynch pointed out in *The Good Funeral: Death, Grief, and the Community of Care,* the idea of "dealing with death by dealing with the dead" had "worked for humans for forty or fifty thousand years all over the planet, across every culture." But more recently, how we deal with death, at least in Western cultures, has changed dramatically. As they explain, "[T]he most recent generation of North Americans . . . , for the past forty or fifty years, have begun to avoid and outsource and ignore their obligation to deal with the dead . . . And a failure to deal authentically with death may have something to do with an inability to deal authentically with life.[10]

According to Long and Lynch,

> Funerals have become increasingly joyful, more
> like celebrations of life than solemn observances of
> death, and nothing is more disruptive to these upbeat
> ceremonies than the morbid presence of a dead body.
> Dead bodies are not emotionally buoyant, and they place
> a drag on the light banter, jokes, laugher and storytelling
> prized in a contemporary service of memory.[11]

"Bright-siding" is a common issue among my clients. One of them was Nick, whose wife urged him to see me. She was worried about his lack of emotion after his brother, Thomas, was killed in a traffic accident.

"I get where she's coming from," Nick told me. "My brother was my best friend, and I can't imagine life without him. But I don't want people to feel sorry for me. I'm a positive person, and I'm not going to let this drag me down. Thomas wouldn't have wanted that."

Here is how Nick spoke of his loss:

> "It was a horrible accident, but at least he didn't have to suffer."

> "Losing my brother is hard, but it is not like losing a child."

> "I really missed Thomas today, but my faith tells me he is in a better place."

In our second session, I suggested there might be a connection between his characteristic positivity and an inability to feel his loss.

"Nothing you've said is not true," I said. "Your brother didn't suffer. The loss of a child is different. I'm sure your faith is a comfort. But you also can't deny this: losing your brother is just really hard."

I asked Nick to slowly repeat the three sentences I listed above but to stop before the word *but*. I encouraged him to feel the feelings brought up by the first part of those sentences. He was extremely reluctant but finally did as I suggested. Then he began to weep.

"Your grief is about how much you love your brother," I told him. "There is nothing negative in that."

From an early age, we learn the dos and don'ts of feelings in our culture. Some degree of socialization is clearly necessary for society to function. Imagine a world in which we all blurt out every thought and express every feeling. But we take this socialization to an extreme by labeling some feelings as "negative."

Many years ago, I witnessed the power of this socialization firsthand. After the tragic death of a local kindergarten child, I was asked to consult with the principal, teachers, and parents of the other children. I helped them come up with this plan: We would leave the deceased student's desk as it had been. Young classmates were invited to bring toys and tokens to place on the desk. Most did. The children also were invited to talk about their missing friend. When I checked in with the teacher, she was amazed by how openly, authentically, and without fear or shame her students expressed their loss. The children were quick to recall their classmate's favorite toy or something funny that happened to him on the playground or the games they played at his last birthday party. There was an innocent beauty in how they expressed their grief.

The very next spring, the same school suffered another terrible tragedy—the sudden death of a second grader. When I was asked to return, I encouraged the community to replicate what we had done after the earlier death. This time, the grieving children responded much differently. Most would not speak of their dead classmate and avoided the student's desk. Absenteeism was up, as were requests to see the school nurse. What a difference just two years of socialization had made.

To once again quote Fred Rogers: "There's no 'should' or 'should not' when it comes to having feelings. They're part of who we are and their origins are beyond our control. When we can believe that, we may find it easier to make constructive choices about what to do with those feelings."[12]

As a therapist, I was trained that actions are negotiable but feelings are not. The kindergarten students could still spontaneously express what they felt. Even though the second graders had the same feelings and stories about their loss as the younger children had and even though they had the encouragement to express those feelings, they had already learned to internalize, which was right on schedule in terms of socialization. No wonder all the trips to the nurse with sore tummies.

In the fall of 1996, I was privileged to witness another example of pure, unsocialized grief. It was my good fortune to become acquainted with Henri Nouwen, the Dutch Catholic priest, writer, and theologian. Henri had spent the last decade of his life as pastor at L'Arche Daybreak, a residential facility in Ontario, Canada, for profoundly mentally challenged adults. While there, he provided pastoral care for this amazing community of residents and helpers.

That fall, some friends and I had planned to meet Henri for a short retreat at L'Arche. But then we learned of his death from a heart attack a few weeks before we were to leave for Canada. We decided to proceed with the visit to L'Arche to mourn Henri in the place that had meant so much to him. However, I was not at all prepared for the environment of grieving that I found there.

In the middle of a meal, a resident would yell, "Henri's dead! Remember to pray for Henri." In the midst of Mass, another resident would shout again, "Henri's dead," which would precipitate loud wailing among the others. The adult residents of L'Arche were like those kindergarten students—transparent and unashamed. They could not *not* express their loss. I have to admit that it was initially unnerving. But I came to appreciate the beauty and power of what I experienced there. What a different, kinder, emotionally healthier world it would be if we could be more like those kindergarten students and the residents of L'Arche.

Instead, the bereaved are more typically treated like C.S. Lewis's lepers. As O'Rourke and Granek wrote in *Slate*:

> Acknowledgement, love, a receptive ear, help with the cooking, company—these were the basic supports that mourning rituals once provided; even if we've never experienced a loss ourselves, we know from literature and history that people require them. Yet as American culture has become divorced from death and dying, we no longer know how to address the most rudimentary aspects of another's loss—*what* to say, *when* to say it, *how* to say it. Disconcerted by discomfort, friends or colleagues are all too likely to disappear or turn the conversation to small talk in the aftermath of a loss, not knowing what to say. Our survey-takers reported wanting to grieve communally and yearning to find ways to relate to those around them.[13]

THE EXPECTATIONS OF OTHERS

Amother who lost her baby son to SIDS just a few days before is told by a woman at the visitation, "Aren't we lucky we had him as long as we did?"

"I'm feeling anything but lucky," the mother responds.

A man who has just lost his father to a sudden heart attack is approached the next day by an old friend who says, "How you doing, Carl? Good?"

Carl hesitates before answering.

"Well, things are kind of tough right now," he says.

A client who just buried his teenage son after a car accident is told by a man, who recently lost an uncle, "I know exactly what you're going through." My client was speechless.

Another client turns down a dinner invitation from a friend because it coincides with the six-month anniversary of her husband's death.

"You're still feeling bad?" the friend says. "Don't you think it's time you got out and started doing things again?"

In our culture, unfortunately, most people don't understand that loss and grief are things to be incorporated into our lives, not things we get past or get over. As chapter 2 explored in depth, our cultural expectations around grief can be unrealistic and harmful. Within days of your loss, you must reengage with society and pretend to feel better than you actually do so that others don't feel awkward. People you thought you could count on to support you suddenly disappear. And day after day, you must endure the misguided comments from well-meaning people who just don't have a clue.

Many clients seek me out because they have felt hurt or abandoned by their community. With family, friends, coworkers, and clergy members—however you choose to define your community—the griever will encounter people who fall into a few categories. There are those who say just the right thing; others who are well meaning but stumble because they don't know better; and others who say or do things that are deeply hurtful. This is all part of your story. It's unrealistic to expect that some social part of your grief would not be challenging or hurtful.

We're all imperfect human beings. In this area, it's important that we offer other people and ourselves some grace. Some are fortunate to possess "grief literacy." They've studied mourning and have learned how to support the bereaved in the most helpful and meaningful ways. Often they have experienced loss themselves. But in our culture, these people tend to be in the minority.

Most of the world—especially younger people—have not experienced wrenching loss. When they encounter those who mourn, they don't know what to say, so they fall back on the culture of positivity or what they've heard other places. If you've heard someone say, "He's in a better place," you're likely to repeat it. You wouldn't naturally understand that being with a grieving person is more important and helpful than trying to make a grieving person feel better. The point is to be with them in their sadness.

There is often a profound difference between those who have suffered a loss and those who haven't. If you are thirty-five years old and your grandparents are still alive, no wonder you are anxious and tongue-tied around a friend who has just lost a child. But someday you will know what the sorrow of loss feels like. Many clients tell me that they support other grieving friends much differently after having grieved themselves.

"I listen better."

"I don't speak in clichés. I didn't know what that felt like until I was on the receiving end of them."

"I'm totally okay when people need to cry."

We need to do better as a culture. The lack of grief fluency and understanding, in addition to harmful theories, drives grievers underground and into isolation with their feelings, creating added layers of self-doubt and shame.

Most grieving people are surrounded by others with varying degrees of "grief literacy." Some have suffered a loss themselves and know what it's like to mourn. Or they are naturally compassionate, intuitive people who are not afraid to get close to human suffering and can do so without feeling like they need to fix it. They instinctively know what to say.

Then there are the others who, for any number of reasons (including those I just mentioned), assume they know what you're feeling, promote the idea of closure, or fall back on platitudes like "be strong" or "count your blessings" or remind you that "time heals all wounds" or that "God doesn't give us any more than we can handle." Supporters think they are helping a mourning person by trying to make him or her feel better, to "cheer them up." Or they may be uncomfortable around anguish and fall back on clichés to manage their own fear and awkwardness.

Whatever the reasons, at a time when the bereaved need to be supported wherever they are, they instead must listen to comments that are irrelevant and often contradictory to how they feel or what they need. They may get irritated and angry but typically try not to show it. Or they may slough it off, knowing that the hurt wasn't intentional. Or, most problematically, the insensitive comments cause them to doubt their feelings and experience.

So I urge you: Do not let what you hear or the opinions of others dictate your own inner reality. Be aware of situations when the words of supporters do not attune with your feelings or thinking. Don't change your story. Be unyielding about that. Try to remind yourself that some people are well meaning but are not fluent in grief, have no experiences with loss themselves, or are just plain scared. Try not to invest much energy in those interactions.

You also always have choices about how to respond. One is to be gracious and merely say, "Thank you for your support." You are also entitled to tell the truth: "I know you mean well, but I don't really feel like counting my blessings right now. I'm in too much pain," or "With all due respect, I don't think you know what I'm going through."

The situation is more easily managed at the visitation and funeral, with people you might never see again. But what if the offending person is the next-door neighbor or your mother-in-law who continues to try to steer you to the bright side? You may have to assert yourself. "I know you want me to see the silver lining, but that's not where I am right now. What I need is for you to accept me where I am and stop judging my feelings."

The mother-in-law either gets it, or she doesn't. If she is offended ("I was only trying to help"), there is nothing you can do. Try not to take it personally. She is likely insensitive with most people. Continue to seek out those with whom you feel emotionally safe.

It's very important to understand that the experience of loss in a faith community may be unquestioningly supportive or surprisingly disappointing. We might hold higher expectations for support from those in our faith community. But, in truth, the same spectrum of support—or lack of it—is typically found in religious groups. At the wake, we might expect some insensitivity from a coworker or casual acquaintance, while expecting much more from a person who has been part of our Bible study class for a decade. And yet, there is no reason to assume that everyone in our religious community will get it right. But when they don't, it seems that the potential for hurt and disappointment is magnified.[1]

When members of a faith community get it wrong, it can strike a deeper chord because of the implication that you are not living up to your faith or that grieving is somehow contrary to faith. This situation creates a dilemma: either you must push back and defend your feelings, or you must agree with the community and begin to doubt your own faith and yourself. And even if you do believe that God had a purpose for taking your baby, that does not mean you don't get to be sad.

Many people in a religious community are everything a grieving person could hope for, providing nonjudgmental companionship over the long haul. But even these people in the faith community may drop away from the griever as quickly as people in the secular world. There are all variations in between.

Religious clichés are particularly common and are rarely helpful. In the case of death—in particular, sudden death—doubt is normal. "Why did this happen? I am so angry at God! If there is a God, how could he allow this?" The best response would be, "I get it. Of course you're doubting right now. Anyone would be." That's very different from, "We can't question God's will," or "Everything happens for a reason," or "God called him home." Faithful people have doubts after loss, but the lack of support within their faith community adds another layer of shame.

My client Vickie and her brother, Perry, were both grateful that their conversion to Christianity in their adolescent years had delivered them from the horrors of an alcoholic home. As an adult, Vickie attended Bible studies, taught Sunday school, and volunteered for overseas mission trips. When Perry was diagnosed with cancer, both he and his sister believed God would save him again, but it wasn't to be. Vickie's faith was shattered when Perry died, and she made the mistake of saying so at a Bible study.

"I said that I couldn't help wondering if there really was a God," she told me. "At first there was silence. Then they all started reciting scripture, telling me Perry's death was part of a divine plan and that he was in a better place. I felt ashamed for doubting."

Vickie found a support group outside of church, where members had experienced similar doubts and freely shared them.

Her crisis of faith eventually passed. In our last session, she told me that she had begun to volunteer as a lay visitor to the bereaved in their congregation.

"When people are hurting, they don't need theology," she said. "They just need to be heard."

Joanne had just lost her baby to SIDS when she heard this from an aunt, a person of spiritual authority in her life: "God must have needed your baby more than you did. God called your baby home."

Joanne, a deeply religious person herself, didn't know how to respond.

"I guess so," she said meekly. But she was devastated.

"Did God need my baby more than I did?" she asked me in our first session. "Did I do something wrong? Was I a bad mother?"

I could assure her that she was not, that the problem was with the insensitive words of her aunt. Joanne tried to avoid her aunt from then on.

If what you hear after a loss does not match your internal experience, no matter how steeped the words might be in religious authority, trust your internal experience. I know how difficult that will be for many. When your emotional experience does not line up with what you believe or what you are told you should believe, this becomes part of your grief story, too.

It's important to understand why you're confused. Anyone in the same situation would be. Don't run from this feeling.

Share your true feelings and doubts with a faithful person who you know from experience you can trust. This will take discernment. Avoid people who you don't feel safe with when discussing faith questions.

Just remember: your feelings are never wrong, and your sadness is not negotiable. In my mind, nothing in the authentic experience of grief, sadness, anger, or doubt is incompatible with faith.

≋

The culture of positivity can also lead people to say insensitive, unhelpful things to the bereaved. It took me many weeks to convince Martha, whose best friend had been killed in a traffic accident, that her profound sorrow did not mean she was weak or wallowing or being negative, despite what her family was telling her.

Martha was a product of her upbringing. Her grandfather built a business empire by channeling positive thoughts into profitable action. The family's feel-good platitudes continued, even after Martha's terrible loss.

"At least she didn't have to suffer," one family member told her.

"It's lucky she didn't have children," said another.

Our first session was taken up by Martha's shame. In her second visit, she started back in with the self-recrimination.

"Could we take a few minutes so you can tell me about your friend?" I asked. "How did you meet?"

Martha seemed surprised. Then she started telling me about her first day at college. Her roommate had been unpacking when Martha got to her dorm room.

"The first thing she did was share this huge bag of peanut M&Ms," Martha said. "It was like we had known each other all our lives. We communicated with each other at least once a week since we graduated. I even started to call her the other day."

She began to weep. I reassured her that her tears were about love, not negativity. Martha came to understand that feelings are just feelings and that sadness was just as valuable as joy.

In our next sessions, I encouraged Martha to continue telling her story of love for her friend. I told her that she could choose to avoid her well-meaning but unhelpful family and instead find friends who allowed her to express her grief. She could also choose to assert herself more with her family.

Martha did begin to push back against her family, which is something we discussed at length in our sessions. She felt like she had no choice but to do so. Once she learned the truth about grief and feelings, she could no longer tolerate an environment in which everything was spun toward the positive. She needed to set boundaries with that behavior and remain true to herself.

"I'm not feeling grateful that she didn't suffer," she would tell her family. "I'm feeling sad that I lost her."

A family member would challenge her by saying, "Why do you look so sad? It's a beautiful day." Martha would reply, "It is a beautiful day, and my sadness doesn't change that one bit. I'm sad. That's not negative."

It was frustrating to her family and some relationships suffered, but it was more important to Martha that she remain true to herself and honor her dead friend by grieving fully. This experience helped her be a more authentic human being, and she defended that authenticity in her family, though it wasn't always pleasant. Once again, you're sad because you're attached, not because you're negative.

As I said at the beginning of this chapter, grieving people must be great actors by necessity. They are forced into an exhausting charade within a few days of a loss. As they reengage with society, the bereaved don't want to be the source of awkwardness in social, work, and family situations, so they act better than they feel. I refer to this as *social splitting*.

Linda, a supervisor in the aerospace industry, came to me after losing her mother to Alzheimer's disease. She appreciated the cards and flowers and expressions of concern from coworkers, but the condolences stopped within days, and Linda expected nothing less. She and her coworkers had important work to do.

But she noticed that her mind kept wandering in meetings. She hoped her coworkers didn't notice the redness in her eyes after crying jags in a restroom stall. She came to me because of the fear that her distraction might actually be jeopardizing her career.

"How much of your day do you spend acting better than you feel?" I asked.

She thought and then responded, "The only time I can stop pretending is after my husband goes to bed."

For Linda, that turned out not to be enough. At my suggestion, every evening after her husband retired for the day, she took time to sit with her grief. She would go through old photographs, journal, call up an old friend to share memories of her mother, or just sit with her feelings in a quiet house. It became sacred time for her each day. At work, when she felt overwhelmed by the heaviness, she could say to herself, "Tonight I will have my time with Mom."

The bereaved also must contend with personal disappointment when people they expected to lean on suddenly disappear. My client Brad was one of them.

Brad's teenage son was killed in a hunting accident. One of Brad's first calls was to Chris, his best friend from college and best man at his wedding. Their sons had been born within a year of each other, and when the boys were older, the four of them took regular ski trips.

After the tragedy, Chris attended the funeral but never called afterward.

"I thought about calling him, but that seemed backward," Brad told me. "I mean, I was the one who lost a son. It got to the point where I wondered whether something had happened to Chris."

Another fraternity brother eventually explained Chris's silence.

"Chris started to cry on the phone when this other guy brought up my name," Brad said. "Chris told him, 'I don't do death. And I can't stop thinking that it could have been my son who was killed.'"

Brad was devastated.

"If it had been his son, I would have sucked it up and been there for him, no matter what," he said.

But how would he approach his relationship with Chris moving forward? I recommended that he think through his choices and decide whether he would invest any more energy in the friendship. Brad decided he would not attempt to contact Chris and was comfortable with the possibility of never speaking to him again.

"What happens if he comes back around in a year and acts as if nothing had happened?" I asked him. "Are you willing to pick up with the friendship?"

"No way," Brad said. "I would feel like I betrayed myself and my son."

"If we're going to be friends, we need to talk about this," Brad said. "He would need to know how I felt when he disappeared.

And I would have to hear from him that he was sorry for how he acted."

Very few of my clients in similar situations have said they could later act as if nothing had happened. Therefore, I would recommend the same course of action to you when close friends or relatives let you down in your time of need. You don't have to be belligerent or aggressive. However, if a relationship is to continue, it's important to convey the depth of your confusion, disappointment, and sadness at the behavior of another who clearly failed you.

Friendships can end because of this. I'll often hear people say, "I'll keep her as a friend, but I won't open up to her like I used to. I'm not going to talk to her about my loss."

Painful circumstances are often revelatory, showing you a side of people you had not seen before. You don't have to understand why people do what they do, but you do have to trust what your intuition and experience are telling you.

Vickie decided to stay in her church but changed her behavior there. Joanne tried to keep distance from her aunt. Brad decided to end his friendship with Chris and said he would insist on honesty if the friend resurfaced. It was not easy for any of these three people, but each of them remained true to themselves. The alternative would have been much worse.

Finally, there are those who are tirelessly helpful and supportive but for all the wrong reasons. And motives matter. A bereaved person will eventually be able to tell whether a person is there to support them or to fulfill their own deep need to be needed. These kinds of folks can be more difficult for the bereaved than an overtly clueless person.

Tad and Maria came to see me after their daughter was killed in a car accident. I was surprised when an early session was taken up by discussion of Maria's friend, Betty.

Betty had been at the family home within minutes of learning of the tragedy and was at Maria's side throughout the visitation and funeral. But Maria began to notice that she was more tense and weary when Betty was around. When she wanted to lie down for a nap, she couldn't because Betty was hovering. Betty seemed oblivious to the couple's need for space. She was offended when the couple didn't acknowledge her efforts organizing meals or when Maria didn't thank her for running an errand.

"I appreciate everything you've done," Maria said finally. "But frankly, making sure you feel appreciated just isn't a priority right now. We need some privacy and don't feel like talking. It doesn't seem like you understand what we need."

Betty gathered up her things. "Some thanks," she said.

Tad and Maria felt bad about hurting her feelings, but both were glad to see her go. This was confusing to them, and they felt they had done something wrong. I explained that although Betty was masquerading as the ideal helper, she really wasn't. Her support was not about what the grieving couple needed; it was about her own need to be recognized. That was the dominant factor.

This is an important scenario that I rarely see discussed. A person who is more overtly insensitive is much easier to identify than a self-centered person pretending to be a helper. Here are some ways to tell one from the other.

A true helper is humble, doesn't ask for anything, and doesn't need to be recognized for what they do. They ask what your needs are and don't assume to know. Again, trust what your intuition is telling you. If you recognize that you're spending energy to make a helper feel good about the help they give, there is a problem. People like that can be a real energy drain at a time when energy is at a premium. Ask yourself whether a person gives you energy by their help or saps it.

Setting boundaries with these folks can be awkward, but you may have to be assertive and speak up when someone has over-stepped. Don't accept offers of help just so others will feel better about themselves.

If you are grieving now, it is likely that you have endured people who, perhaps unintentionally, have said or done insensitive things that have been hurtful, irritating, or exhausting. That experience with others, both the good and the bad, and how you felt about it are important parts of your third chapter of grief. Although you might not have been able to openly express your hurt with that person, you can in your story. Go to your journal and be honest there. Your feelings deserve to be acknowledged.

Journaling allows us to sort through all the feelings that come up when someone says something insensitive to us. It also affords us the opportunity to express on the page the things we felt we couldn't say in person or just couldn't find words to express at the time. As one example of a journal entry, write a letter to that person that you will never send. This can often help you come to terms with the loss within the loss.

Finally, you have every right to avoid people who have said misguided or cruel words to you. Even if you are fully aware that they mean well, and even if you understand that they are operating under unhelpful expectations when it comes to grief, you still are entitled to grieve in your own way and to feel what you feel without enduring others' judgments and platitudes. In the face of loss, your only obligation is to take care of your own heart—not the feelings, beliefs, or egos of others.

HELP FOR THE HELPER

Most people want to support a grieving person in truly meaningful ways. If you are one of them, you might now feel remorse for having inadvertently hurt a grieving friend with something you said or did not say, something you did or did not do. If you had known better, you would have done better. You will know better now.

Let me begin by addressing the question that most haunts those about to encounter a grieving person: "What should I say?"

Here is the answer: "I'm very sorry."

That's all that is necessary. Really. Just mean it and then be quiet—even if you are so desperate to be helpful that you just want to keep talking.

Here's what *not* to do.

- Don't assume your experience or religious beliefs will be relevant to a bereaved person or that he or she needs educating about grief.

- Don't question the length or intensity of a person's grief, which might imply that a person is grieving in a "wrong" way.

- Don't assume that your grief experience is the same as the bereaved person's, and never compare one loss to another.

- Don't compliment the bereaved about their strength or courage or tell them they seem to be "holding up well." Appearances can be deceiving, and saying this could create an expectation that they *should* be "doing well." That, in turn, could drive their true feelings underground.

- Don't give advice unless it is specifically requested. Our usual inclination when we hear a problem or someone in distress is to assume that advice is being asked for. Instead, I suggest the following listening rule: never give advice and you will rarely be wrong in your response.

- And finally, avoid clichés.

The following are the most common clichés, separated into three groups. This first group implies that there should be a timetable for grief.

"Time heals all wounds."

"You have to move on."

"Grief happens in stages."

"I hope you find closure."

The next clichés are by-products of our culture of positivity.

"Be strong."

"He wouldn't want you to be sad."

"It's important to stay busy and productive."

"You can't dwell in the past."

"Count your blessings."

"Others have it worse."

"This will make you stronger."

"You seem to be holding up really well."

"Look for the silver lining."

"I know just how you feel."

"You have your whole life ahead of you."

"At least you're young enough to have another child/remarry."

Finally, religious platitudes imply that a faithful person should not mourn.

"God doesn't give you more than you can handle."

"God has a plan."

"Everything happens for a reason."

"He/she is in a better place."

"It was her/his time to go."

"My thoughts and prayers are with you" might not be a cliché per se, but it is uttered so often that the words have lost meaning. The same is true for, "Let me know if there is anything I can do." The offer is rarely sincere, and a grieving person knows it. Comedian George Carlin imagined a bereaved person replying, "Yeah, you can come over this weekend and paint my garage."

If you want to help, be specific and follow through. Arrange meals, transport children, or mow the grass. A friend shared this story of a family doctor in a small town in the Midwest. Whenever a death occurred, the doctor would come knocking at the door of the bereaved. He was there to collect the shoes to be worn for the funeral.

"I'll polish them and have them back to you in plenty of time," the doctor said.

As the shoes were gathered up, he would sit, listen, and console and then head off with his bag of shoes. The doctor, his wife, and children would polish and buff and carefully wrap the shoes in butcher paper to be dropped off the next morning. It got to the point that the doctor no longer needed to ask. Unpolished shoes would be waiting for him on the front porch whenever there was a death. Everyone knew that he would be by to pick them up.

I still feel gratitude for our friends who, after our son died, put a trip together to the mountains to get us out of town so we could rest from the long and intense nine months we had experienced. They knew just what to do for us.

To be a true comfort, you must be able to meet the grieving person wherever they are, even if you find their behavior foreign to your experience or personal comfort. The charming little movie *Lars and the Real Girl* has much to teach in that regard.

The title character is a withdrawn and socially impaired young man who lives in a small Wisconsin town. His parents are dead, so he lives in the garage apartment owned by his brother and sister-in-law, who watch out for him. Lars is terrified of intimacy and keeps mostly to himself.

Then, on a whim, Lars orders a life-sized female doll from an adult website, calling her Bianca. Their relationship is chaste but intimate. Lars finally has someone he can talk to. Their bond is such that Lars asks his brother if he can bring a date to dinner. The brother is delighted at the prospect but is then shocked when Lars walks in carrying a life-size doll.

The town doctor is consulted and suggests that the best thing for Lars is for the town to treat Bianca as if she were real, allowing time for Lars's fantasy to run its course. The happy couple pop up all over and are greeted warmly. For the first time in his life, Lars feels like he is part of the community.

But then his love affair takes a tragic turn. In Lars's fantasy, Bianca comes down with a terminal illness. Women bring their knitting and food to Bianca's death vigil.

"We brought casseroles," they tell Lars.

"Is there something I should be doing?" he asks.

"No, dear," one lady responds. "Just eat. That's what people do when tragedy strikes. They come over and sit."

At Bianca's funeral, the small town church is full.

Broken down, the word *compassion* means "to suffer with" (*com* means "with" and *passion* means "to suffer"). Supporting a bereaved person means just that—deciding to enter into their pain.

According to Henri Nouwen,

> Compassion asks us to go where it hurts, to enter into the places of pain, to share in brokenness, fear, confusion, and anguish. Compassion challenges us to cry out in misery, to mourn with those who are lonely, to weep with those in tears. Compassion requires us to be weak with the weak, vulnerable with the vulnerable, and powerless with the powerless. Compassion means full immersion in the condition of being human.[1]

This is a tall order if ever there was one. How, exactly, do you show true compassion for a grieving person? Here are a few ideas.

Show up at the house, visitation, or funeral; express simple words of sorrow; and then let the mourning person dictate what happens next. She may open her arms for a hug, or she may clearly want to keep people at a distance. He may be calm or agitated. She may be jovial or weeping. He may want to talk about his loss or about baseball. She may be angry or grateful. Be with them wherever they are.

I define intimacy as truly knowing another person and being known. Being with a person in grief is a unique, one-way intimacy. You are there to know the grieving person but not to fix or make him or her feel better. Don't try to move the bereaved from one emotional place to another to make yourself more comfortable. Be with them without an agenda. You may be more comfortable with a person's anger than with their silence, or you may rather talk about sports than the accident—but this isn't about you.

Listen with your eyes and respond with nods that convey, "I get it."

Laugh with them when it's time to laugh. Cry if tears come. Be like Bob.

I learned about Bob from my client, Casey, an intensely shy man of forty who was overwhelmed by the attention he received after the death of his mother.

"The night after she died, there was huge crowd at the house. Every time I turned around, someone wanted to hug me," Casey told me. "Most people know I hate that, but I guess they figured that under the circumstances, it would be different. It got to where I would step away from people when they put their arms out."

Bob, his old friend, was different.

"The moment I saw him, I relaxed," Casey said. "He just stuck out his hand and told me he was sorry. Then he drifted off so someone else could say hello. A little while later, I noticed Bob standing by himself, sipping a soda, like he was biding his time. After a few minutes, he came over and said: 'It's kind of stuffy in here. How about some air?' He realized before I did that the walls were closing in."

"We went out back and sat on a couple of lawn chairs," Casey continued. "I swear, he never said a word. We just sat there looking at the stars and listening to the wind. I think Bob knew I was overwhelmed with words by that point. The next thing I knew, I started to cry. He reached over and patted me on the back, but it was no big deal. After a few minutes, I said, 'I guess I can go back in now.' He said, 'I'll be around.'"

"He still makes a point of calling or sending me an email every so often," Casey said. "We've spent a few nights out back, drinking beer. He never says all that much, just listens when I talk about my mom or whatever else is going on."

Bob is a fine example of "companioning," a wonderful verb coined by Alan Wolfelt, one of our leading writers on the topic of supporting the bereaved.

> Companioning is about being present to another person's pain; it is not about taking away the pain.

> Companioning is about going to the wilderness of the soul with another human being; it is not about thinking you are responsible for finding the way out.

> Companioning is about honoring the spirit; it is not about focusing on the intellect.

> Companioning is about listening with the heart; it is not about analyzing with the head.

> Companioning is about bearing witness to the struggles of others; it is not about judging or directing these struggles.

> Companioning is about walking alongside; it is not about leading or being led.

> Companioning means discovering the gifts of sacred silence; it does not mean filling up every moment with words.

> Companioning is about being still; it is not about frantic movement forward.

Companioning is about respecting disorder and confusion; it is not about imposing order and logic.

Companioning is about learning from others; it is not about teaching them.

Companioning is about curiosity; it is not about expertise.[2]

Neuroscience now confirms what those of us in the counseling field have long known—listening with deep attention and compassion literally changes something in the brain of the person being heard. Psychotherapy is, in fact, described by one researcher as "a specific kind of enriched environment designed to enhance the growth of neurons and the integration of neural networks."[3]

In *Social Intelligence,* Daniel Goleman said:

> Full listening maximizes the physiological synchrony, so that emotions align. Such synchrony was discovered during psychotherapy at moments when clients felt most understood by their therapists . . . Intentionally paying attention to someone may be the best way to encourage the emergence of rapport. Listening carefully, with undivided attention, orients our neural circuits for connectivity, putting us on the same wavelength.[4]

Mourners crave that shared wavelength, especially when their brains may be disoriented and chaotic, flooded with thoughts and feelings. You do not have to be a trained therapist to connect to the wavelength of the bereaved. But how can you listen this way?

The key is to be fully present and in the moment. Empty your head and heart and be focused on the person who is speaking, without judgment. This is very hard to do. It takes discipline and practice. Their words inevitably bring up your own thoughts and feelings that cry out to be expressed. Even if you want to offer feedback, don't do it—unless a grieving person asks.

We are all quite accomplished at "pseudo-listening"—looking attentive but thinking about an email that needs sending or groceries that need to be purchased for dinner or the rapidly approaching work deadline. Be aware of when you are pseudo-listening and bring your attention back to the present.

We can lose focus if what is being said makes us uncomfortable. Be aware of the discomfort and remind yourself of the important purpose that your presence serves. The words *attunement* and *mirroring* best describe this type of listening. As John Prendergast explained, "By attune, I mean to accurately sense and resonate with, as when a string on one guitar begins to vibrate in harmony with a string that has been plucked on another guitar."[5]

As we become attuned to ourselves, we can attune to those we sit with in their loss. This may not be easy. It is perfectly normal to feel anxious when in the presence of emotional pain. I still do at times, even after three decades of being with the bereaved. Breathing into and through that anxiety will help you in the attunement process. Our anxiety about being with the bereaved comes from a good place—it signifies our ability to take in and mirror another's sorrow. It means that, at some level, we may feel what the bereaved person is feeling. It takes conscious effort on the part of the supporter to first be aware of that anxiety and to then push through it to remain present. Doing so is certainly contrary to our instincts for seeking pleasure and avoiding pain. But intellectually we can assure ourselves that pain is serving a higher purpose, and we will not be damaged by it.

Much like a mother who mirrors the expressions of her infant, thereby creating a deep bond, the bereaved also seek mirroring and connection, or attunement, in their sorrow.

Try this exercise, one I learned in training. Find a television news or talk show and listen to one sentence, then mute the sound and repeat the sentence out loud. Try two sentences, three sentences, and so on. Notice how quickly you form opinions about what you hear. Notice how easily you become distracted by other mental chatter. Keep at the exercise, focusing on the sentences. This will help you develop your listening muscles.

It is when you are truly listening that you can most effectively validate the words of the bereaved person, and validation is the whole point. Again, never challenge sadness, anger, fear, happiness, or confusion. Validation means offering nonjudgmental nods of the head and words of encouragement that say, in effect, "I understand how you would feel that way."

For those who mourn, the wake and funeral service are often blurs of adrenaline. The true pain of bereavement typically comes later, after the funeral, when the last casserole dish has been returned and ordinary life resumes. Love and compassion thus have the most impact on the days, weeks, months, and years to come.

Here are some ideas for supporting a grieving person over the longer term. Some of them are from my own experience—little things that were meaningful to me or that I wish someone had done for me as I've grieved for Ryan. Some are things clients have told me meant a lot to them or would mean a lot to them.

- Bring a meal on the two-month anniversary of a death.

- Send an email to say you were thinking about the grieving person or the one they lost.

- Call and leave a message. A quick text could mean everything, especially if it is received on a particularly difficult day.

- When you are with the bereaved person, say the name of the one they lost. Grieving people love hearing it from the lips of someone else.

- Don't assume there is a timeline to grief. An email a year after a loss could be more meaningful than one a week later.

- Remember the bereaved on holidays, birthdays, anniversaries, or any day that you know has special meaning.

- Offer to visit, but always let the choice be that of the bereaved person. Offer, "I completely understand if the timing is not good."

- Don't assume that a bereaved person has sufficient emotional support. For example, family members often have a hard time supporting each other. As we've seen, each will grieve very differently and will often be incapable of taking care of anyone but him- or herself. Consider trying this: you and a group of friends could coordinate how each of you will support a different member of a grieving family.

- Be curious about the grieving person's relationship to the one they lost. Try asking some of the questions from earlier in this book or one of the following:
  › "I don't know how you and Suzy met. Can you tell me?"
  › "I know the two of you loved to travel. What was your favorite trip?"
  › "What do you miss most about him?"
  › "How are you doing today?"
  › "We've never really talked about the day it happened. I'd like to hear about it if you're able."
  › "I am sorry I did not get to meet your dad. I would love for you to tell me about him."

- Bring up your own memories: "Remember that time we double-dated in college?" or "You may not know this, but your dad was a big influence on my life."

- Offer to listen to a grieving person's story. Tell them that this book taught you the importance of that listening, however they want to share it. A bereaved person might be looking for a safe set of ears, a place for the story to land. That could be you.

Remember the words of Shakespeare: "Give sorrow words; the grief that does not speak / Whispers the o'er-fraught heart and bids it break." Make room in your own heart to let the bereaved "give sorrow words."

Above all, make sure they know that the one they lost has not been forgotten.

13

SORROWS SHARED

Tim Madigan and I have been close friends for many years, but ours had never been a friendship of the golf course or hunting trips or sports talk. Instead, in regular visits at lunch or over coffee, we are more likely to discuss the joys and challenges of manhood, parenting, marriage, and relationships. We've spoken often of our shared love of the mountains and nature, of spirituality, and, yes, of sorrow and loss. It was more than a decade ago that Tim and I first started talking about the possibility of a book about my new way of thinking about grief. He was the one who convinced me that the story of our loss of Ryan should be central to it.

But our kinship runs even deeper to our shared love and mutual admiration for Henri Nouwen and Fred Rogers, whose names have been referenced in this book several times already. It's not an exaggeration to say that those two men, with their wisdom, compassion, and invitation to human authenticity, are the spiritual godfathers of this book. Henri and Fred, perhaps not surprisingly, were also very close friends themselves.

I was not a close personal friend of Henri's, but on several occasions, I had the privilege to be part of a group that shared time with him during his visits to my city. On one of those occasions, Henri was a guest in our home. As I mentioned earlier, I was very much looking forward to being part of a small group to join Henri for a short retreat in Canada, but his death came a month before it was to take place.

The relationship of Tim and Fred was much closer, a rare and beautiful friendship that lasted from the fall of 1995 until Fred's death from stomach cancer in 2003. To a significant extent, their bond began and was deepened through the pain of loss and sorrows shared.

On an autumn day in 1995, my coauthor sat down with Fred in his Pittsburgh office to interview the children's television icon for a newspaper profile. They discussed Fred's career and the philosophy behind *Mister Rogers' Neighborhood.* But then the conversation took an unexpected turn. Mister Rogers began to share his own story of grief.

A few weeks before, one of his oldest and most important friends, a man named Jim Stumbaugh, had died of cancer. Fred described the origins of their friendship when he was a pudgy, shy freshman in high school and Stumbaugh was the star athlete, honor student, and president of his class. They had not known each other well until Stumbaugh suffered a football injury that required him to be hospitalized, and Fred volunteered to bring the other boy his schoolwork. It was the beginning of a "life-altering friendship," Fred said.

Now, in the wake of his friend's death, Fred remembered Stumbaugh as being "in love with life and with learning."

"You hate to lose such a spirit," Fred told Tim.

Fred spent a half-hour remembering his old friend. Finally, he said, "You're ministering to me, Tim. By listening, you minister to me."

Tim has always felt that their friendship began in that moment. The two stayed in frequent contact over the next eight years and shared deeply with each other until Fred's death in 2003. Tim eventually disclosed to Fred his long struggle with depression and a complicated relationship with his father. The two men spoke often about the illness and death of Tim's brother, Steve. The relationship was remarkable because of its fearlessness, the willingness of Tim and Fred to speak openly of hard things.

It was a sunny Saturday morning—September 21, 1996. Tim had just settled in with a cup of coffee and the sports page in his Texas home when the telephone rang. He was surprised to hear Fred's voice at the other end. Within a few seconds, Tim could tell that his friend was weeping. Fred said he had just learned of Henri Nouwen's death from a heart attack.

"I had to talk to someone who understands how I feel," he said.

After their brief conversation, Tim immediately sat down at his computer and wrote his grieving friend this letter.

> Dearest Fred,
>
> The mystery of life deepens. It has only been a few minutes since you called with the terribly sad news about Henri, and thoughts and feelings are swirling about as they do at a time like this.
>
> I don't know about this business of life and death, Fred. I guess the older I get, the more I realize I'm not meant to know. Goodness is no guarantee of a long, abundant life, and in my limited human comprehension, that seems so unfair.
>
> But then, this morning, I am blessed to share in the grief and pain of a dear friend like you, knowing that the life and work of Henri is so much alive in the relationship of you and me. And I come to realize that love and goodness are indestructible,

utterly indestructible, cannot be reduced by time or death, or any other barriers we humans attempt to impose on those sacred things.

Yes, this life is fragile and, at times, terribly hard. One of the things that most drew me to Henri's writings was his willingness to be vulnerable with his readers, to share not only his joy, but his pain and human brokenness. As you know, I, too, struggle with that on a daily basis.

But life is good. Shortly after we hung up this morning, as I was sitting in a chair contemplating the news about Henri, I heard the song of a bird, very loud through our open windows on a beautiful sunny morning. That bird has probably been singing outside my window for eternity, but it took such a reminder of life's fragility for me to finally listen. Not long after hearing the bird, my son Patrick came bounding into the room to share the joy he felt with a toy he bought yesterday with his own money. I asked him for a hug, and he complied with all the vigor a five-year-old can muster. Fragility, mystery, unspeakable beauty.

I'm glad I was home this morning to share your pain. Thank you for calling. In one of your letters, you put it better than I ever could: "Real friendships work both ways. Your trust confirms my trustworthiness; your love, my loving." Hence, this is a bittersweet day for me—the day the world lost Henri Nouwen in the flesh, and the day I heard a bird sing outside my window on a spectacular autumn morning, the day a true friendship deepened even more.

I close with something that will be familiar to you [from Ralph Waldo Emerson's "Friendship."]

"The moment we indulge our affections, the earth is metamorphosed; there is no winter, and no night; all tragedies, all ennuis, vanish—all duties even; nothing fills the proceeding eternity but the forms all radiant of loving persons. Let the soul be assured that somewhere in the universe it should rejoin its friend, and it would be content and cheerful alone a thousand years."

God bless you and yours.

All my love,

Tim[1]

A movement is afoot, and this book is part of it. Only as we come to appreciate that all humans experience shame, sorrow, self-doubt, anger, fear, confusion, and of course, grief, can we let down our defenses and find true connection to one another. Both Henri and Fred believed that those are actually the things we have most in common. "What is most personal is most universal," Henri famously said.[2]

Yet, for most of our shared existence on this planet, we have endeavored so mightily to conceal those things from each other. To again quote Shakespeare:

All the world's a stage,
And all the men and women merely players;
They have their exits and their entrances,
And one man in his time plays many parts.[3]

That's what's changing. More and more of us now realize that our masks do not always serve us well, particularly when we are grieving. We recognize that when we are at our most vulnerable, we need to be around other people who are just as authentic, who have found the courage to step out from behind theirs.

Since Tim's book was first published in 2006, he has traveled the nation with the message of his friendship with Mister Rogers. He often ends his lectures in the following fashion: "I have a confession to make. I'm a mess. But guess what? You're a mess, too. There is another word for me, and that is human. The good news is that we don't have to be messes alone."

I think there is also a growing appreciation for the art of good listening. One inspiring example are two men in Pennsylvania, Michael Gingerich and Thomas Kaden, who started a nonprofit business called Someone to Tell It To. Since 2012, the two men, both ordained ministers, gave up church work to make themselves available—in person, on the telephone, and via text, email, or Skype—to anyone around the world who needed to be listened to. "We all want and need to be heard, to know that others listen and care. We crave intimacy. We are in a constant search for validation and for our voices to find resonance with the lives of others," they wrote in their book *Someone to Tell It To*.[4] They continued:

> We have seen this need again and again during our
> years—visiting people who have been homebound
> or in hospital rooms, or as we've sat with someone
> grieving the death of a loved one, or comforted
> those in distress, pain, loneliness, or uncertainty. We
> have also experienced this need firsthand as we have
> grappled with our own families' challenges with cancer,
> financial pressures, career directions, and disability. We
> have learned how all of us at times vitally need to be
> heard. We need someone to listen so our struggles and
> questions become shared and not ours alone to bear.[5]

Remember those words as you move forward with your narrative of grief. And remember that although they might not show it, most other people are grieving, too.

≋

As we've noted, more private, introverted people might prefer to hold their stories in their own mind and hearts or in journals and notebooks that only they will read. That is perfectly fine. But Tim's experience with Fred bears witness to the beauty and comfort that so often occur when a grief narrative is shared. We want to be loved, nurtured, supported, and acknowledged—but in the right ways. We do not want to feel isolated and alone. And we know intuitively that by sharing our grief, we open ourselves to the possibility of profoundly nourishing experiences with others. By asking someone to listen to your story of loss, you are actually paying the other person a great compliment. As Fred Rogers told Tim: "Your trust confirms my trustworthiness."

Let me suggest another inventory of sorts. Think of the people in your life with whom you've felt most psychologically safe, the people who really listen, those with whom you felt you could take off your mask and speak the truth of your heart, no matter what it happened to be. Most of us have a Mister Rogers in our own lives—a friend, pastor, coach, teacher, sibling, or grandfather who will listen to us and love us no matter what. In your loss, it's very likely that these people have been a great comfort already.

Now comes the hard part. Tell them about your journey with this book. Ask them to read it. Then ask if they would listen to your story, if they would be your grief companion. Tell them they do not need to try to take away your suffering.

Pure listening is all you're asking for. Maybe it's weekly meetings on a park bench or over coffee in a place conducive to expressing emotion. Your options are limitless.

Yes, there is a risk. There is no guarantee it will not backfire, that your words will not land in the lap of a person incapable of bearing them. If you ask and the person declines due to schedule, emotional discomfort, or fear of what your pain might bring up in them, don't take it personally. Thank them for their honesty. Agreeing to be your companion in your grief is a serious decision, requiring a courageous emotional investment.

But most people will be honored that you asked. I'm betting that, in most cases, it will be a profound human experience for you both. You introverts especially might find confidence in the knowledge that people might actually be longing for an affirmation of their trustworthiness. Sharing your grief will not be a burden; it will be a gift.

Finally, I'd like to suggest support groups as a place for you to tell your story or to find a grief companion. These groups are not hard to find. A quick Internet search with your specific need will give you the resources you need. (For more direction on finding a grief support group, see appendix I. I also hope the study guide included in this book serves as a helpful roadmap for those seeking to find or create a supportive community.)

I have spoken to many support groups over the years, and I am always touched and inspired to be with people who are suffering but also committed to helping others. It is a sacred and hopeful thing to watch a person who was once bent over from pain move into a leadership role in one of these groups. That healing generosity speaks to who we really are as humans.

Support groups offer a beautiful balance between the uniqueness of the individual's grief narrative and the universal experience of loss that joins individual stories into one, the story of humanity. In a support group, all of the usual demographics are checked at the door. Your financial status, gender, ethnicity, and profession are irrelevant. Your pain and a need to be understood are the only requirements for membership.

Grief support groups are organized in several ways. Some meet around the calendar, while others meet in consecutive six-week sessions that often coincide with particularly painful times of year, such as the holidays. Groups can be open to those who have suffered any manner of loss or organized around specific types of death, such as suicide or the death of a child or a spouse.

Meetings are typically limited to an hour or ninety minutes and can be organized around specific topics, a speaker, open sharing, or shared readings. Members are encouraged to share but are not forced to do so. Some sit in support group meetings for weeks and months without saying a word; they simply find safety and comfort in the presence of those who have traveled a similar road. Some groups are moderated by a professional, such as a chaplain or social worker. In many, the group members share the leadership.

It takes courage to go to a support group for the first time, and it takes even more courage to share. I understand how daunting it can be. But just try it once. My hope is that this book will help you find emotional safety and intimacy with another. I have heard many say that they experienced more intimacy in a support group of relative strangers than they did among friends and family. Unlike the world of friends and family, support groups often offer a structure, rules, and an intentionality about listening and safety. They are models for the creation of intimacy for the rest of the community.

Support group members I know generally look forward to their meetings, both to share their latest feelings and experiences in chapter three of their grief story and to support the stories of others. Long and wonderful friendships often result.

My long relationship with one group, The WARM Place, was among my life's greatest privileges. For nineteen years, I trained volunteer facilitators at the nonprofit organization that was created to serve grieving children (more than 35,000 since The WARM Place opened in 1989). The group offers a beautiful opportunity to sit with other kids and trained volunteers where feelings of loss can be listened to and affirmed. The members will carry that experience with them for the rest of their lives. I can only begin to imagine the benefit to our community's mental health.

14

A THERAPIST GRIEVES STILL

I still grieve. I always will, as will you, because we have loved and continue to choose to love.

I am in a season of life in which births and deaths share my emotional landscape. Within three months last year, I experienced the joy of the birth of my youngest grandson and the sorrow of the death of the last living relative in the generation before me. I continue to appreciate how the joy of loving and the sorrow of loss are joined together in the same moment. Loss is unbidden, and yet it always transforms. That is the paradox I have come to understand and deeply appreciate through the years since Ryan died. Loss always beckons me to ask what is important and what is not. Loss invites me to be more present to the relationships I am so grateful for.

In reflecting on my experience of my grief from Ryan's death over the past three decades, I have also come to appreciate the term *shadow grief*. I've often seen this term used to describe the experience of bereaved parents, but I think it applies to many who mourn. Shadow grief is "a dull ache in the background of one's feelings that remains fairly constant and that, under certain circumstances and on certain occasions, comes bubbling to the surface, sometimes in the form of tears, sometimes not, but always accompanied by a feeling of sadness and a mild sense of anxiety."[1]

My grief today is an intermittent ache, not an acute, continuing pain. A peace pervades my sorrow. Gone are the chaotic thoughts and the feelings of darkness that engulfed me in the early years. But even though there is plenty of light, the shadow is just behind me. This book and other writings I have done over the past couple years have inspired many moments when old sorrow bubbles to the surface in the present. I welcome these moments; I appreciate them for rekindling my story of love and loss.

One such moment occurred a couple of years ago, after my wife and one of our friends created a business to capture oral histories on video. Nancy was immediately struck by the beauty and power of the life stories about siblings, parents, spouses, and children. Most of her clients were older people, so the narrative often included memories of loss.

I had long planned to write my own grief story, preserving Ryan's narrative for our children and grandchildren. But Nancy's experience inspired us to preserve those memories in a different way. She wanted our children and grandchildren to know Ryan as more than the brother who died. The time was right to create this video.

Nancy and I sat down in the living room of our home, with Bob, her partner, behind the camera. Just as I have done so many times with my clients, Bob told us to start at the beginning.

We remembered how young we were; we talked of that frightening visit to the doctor's office when labor had begun. We needed little prompting after that, as the memories flowed freely. I would remember something, and Nancy would think of something else. We spoke of Ryan's birth, remembered the six-month stay at the hospital, and recalled the joyful and terrifying ten weeks we spent with our son at home. We remembered all the kind and devoted people at the hospital and how so many dear friends and family members supported us. We remembered our heartache, both at the time of our loss and in all the years to come.

It had been years, maybe decades, since I had spoken of Ryan in that way or that we, as his parents, had a chance to speak of it together in such detail. By then I fully appreciated the value of the story of loss, but rarely had I had the chance to tell my own. As we spoke to the camera, I felt closer to our son than I had in a long time. My bond with Ryan had always been there, but to feel it, sense it, smell it—I could once again touch the fear and the joy, the darkness and the light. Tears came again, after all the years.

The experience of making the video also reminded me how important it is to be able to speak and hear the name of the one who died. Many clients also describe this desire to hear the name of their loved one and the pain when it remains unsaid. In my sessions, I make a point of saying the name of the one who is gone, over and over.

One night last year, I knew we had entered a new stage in our family story. I was standing in the kitchen with my son Kevan, when he said, "I don't know much about Ryan's story. What happened?" It was a milestone moment. Nancy and I had spoken often of Ryan to our sons over the years, as we wanted his place in our family to be honored and for his brothers to understand what they could. But years passed without much mention of the brother they never knew. That night, however, Kevan, an expectant father himself, wanted to hear it with adult ears.

As we stood in the kitchen, I told him the story from beginning to end. He absorbed it in his own quiet way. His response was short, simple, and perfect.

"That must have been hard," he said when I was finished.

I recently sent a message to my youngest son, Connor, who lives out of state, wondering about his thoughts and feelings about Ryan. Because he was a young man who was most at home in nature, I was not surprised to learn that an epiphany about Ryan took place while Connor was camping. Connor wrote in reply:

> I remember knowing about him, but there wasn't much emotion involved until I was older, into my teens. I think that, for a long time, I thought of his death as something similar to a miscarriage, and it wasn't until later that I really understood that he lived for many months and that you and Mom had a long period of caring for him and growing in attachment to him before he died. The most prominent memory by far for me in relation to Ryan happened on one of my solo survival trips. Being alone and hungry already increases the visceral nature of everything, so I was in a somewhat intensified state when I found some photo albums from Ryan's life in the back of the car. I'm not sure why they were in there, but I took some time to look through them.
>
> I had always felt there was a dark cloud or a heavy sadness in you and Mom from Ryan's death, but looking through the photos really gave me an overwhelming feeling of the grief of the whole situation. They were pictures of young, first-time parents who had never loved something so much before. Seeing how tiny and fragile he was and how much you loved him and understanding

that he went through all these complications but survived, even to the point of getting to leave the hospital, made it all sink in for me. Very tough to be out there alone in my wilderness, feeling all of these feelings for the first time, but glad to finally feel like I was seeing you and Mom and understanding what you went through.

These interactions with our adult sons about Ryan caused me to revisit questions I have grappled with periodically over the years. How did the trauma of loss affect the way I parented my two living sons? How did Ryan's loss change our marriage? How did it affect my Christian faith? How did his death change the lives of his grandparents, aunts, uncles, cousins, and our friends? These questions are really not answerable, but they are important. They shine a light on the fragility of life and how sacred stories can change in an instant.

I have taken off work on the anniversary of Ryan's death every year since that first year. I go to the cemetery to think about him and the years now behind me. His grave is close to those of my parents. A generation is missing there: my own. Powerful feelings rise each time I see my son's name on the grave marker: RYAN PALMER O'MALLEY. It grounds me in the hard reality—this really happened. There are other infants buried in the same row of the cemetery. I wonder about their stories and the other bereaved parents who share with us this sacred and solemn piece of earth.

So many memories come flooding back with every moment I stand there. I remember the procession to his grave on that spring day after his funeral. Looking out the car window, I wondered what bystanders might be thinking. We passed a construction site. All the workers removed their hardhats and placed them over their hearts as we drove by. That gesture of honor and respect has stayed with me through the decades. Those workers had no idea what a gift they gave me. They did not know our story, but they did what they knew to do. By doing so, they created a beautiful memory and moment of grace for me. They became part of my story—one unforgettable moment. There will be more. The story continues.

EPILOGUE

On January 10, 2015, I published an essay in the *New York Times* beneath a headline that would later become the title of this book: "Getting Grief Right." From the perspective of a psychotherapist practicing for nearly forty years, I challenged the notion that mourning proceeds predictably and efficiently from one stage to the next or that grievers could expect to reach some psychological finish line, such as acceptance or closure.

That idea "is still deeply and rigidly embedded in our cultural consciousness and psychological language," I wrote.

> It inspires much self-diagnosis and self-criticism among the aggrieved. This is compounded by the often subtle and well-meaning judgment of the surrounding community. A person is to grieve for only so long and with so much intensity.
>
> To be sure, some people who come to see me exhibit serious, diagnosable symptoms that require treatment. Many, however, seek help only because they and the people around them believe that time is up on their grief. The truth is that grief is as unique as a fingerprint, conforms to no timetable or societal expectation.[1]

My editors at the *Times* were amazed by the response. The piece was one of the most widely read stories in that day's paper and inspired nearly four hundred online reader messages. "I've never, ever, seen a piece that inspired more comments that began with 'Thank you,'" one editor said. "The piece was a real service." I also received dozens of letters from around the country from readers and appreciative notes from many prominent members of my field.

"One of my children died of [SIDS] twenty-three years ago, and I wish I had seen the article then!" wrote one reader. "There is so much pressure in our society to be 'better' quickly; it is helpful to realize that there is no one path to grief."

Another reader wrote: "A very thoughtful—and, I hope, helpful—article. My youngest son died in a car crash at age eighteen nearly five years ago. Our culture's metaphors for grieving, such as 'getting over it' and 'moving on' are, in my experience, decidedly unhelpful. I have seen much unnecessary suffering created for people through such notions."

Finally, a reader offered "heartfelt gratitude for this article. My very own therapist has been chiding me for being 'irresponsible' because I've been 'indulging my grief' instead of moving on. 'One year should be the maximum for losing a loved one,' she says. In addition to living with and in grief, I also shoulder the guilt that gets piled on me. It's not a surprise that this therapist has never lost a pet, a parent, a child, or a loved one."

The online comments, personal letters, and phone calls I received in response to my essay were a great encouragement to me to continue on the mission of offering this message about loss and mourning in the form of this book. Although I suspected it was the case from working with grieving clients through the years, I didn't fully appreciate the extent to which so many were isolated in their grief; they often felt shame about their sorrow and desired acknowledgment of their loss. The stories from around the country and overseas also spoke to another undeniable reality—no one escapes grief.

It is my sincere desire that this book has been a help and comfort to you as you walk through the inevitable. No single book could possibly cover every aspect of grieving, but perhaps *Getting Grief Right* has been a useful companion to you in your journey of loss. As you continue your story of love and loss, I wish you peace.

NOTES

Introduction

1. "Talk with Isak Dineson," interview by Bent Mohn, *New York Times Book Review,* November 3, 1957.
2. Anne Lamott, *Plan B: Further Thoughts on Faith* (New York: Riverhead Books, 2006), 174.

Chapter 1: A Therapist Grieves

1. Ruth Davis Konigsberg, *The Truth About Grief* (New York: Simon & Schuster Paperback, 2011), 11.

Chapter 2: The Cage of the Stages

1. Ronald Kotulak, "Scientists Measure 5 Stages of Grief," *Chicago Tribune,* February 21, 2007, articles.chicagotribune.com/2007-02-21news/ 0702210198_1_peak-at-five-months-point-at-four-months-yale-bereavement-study. (Author's note: The opening paragraph of the online version of the article differs slightly from the version I read in my print newspaper, but the facts about the Yale study and the essential information of the article are the same.)
2. Sigmund Freud, "Mourning and Melancholia," in *The Standard Edition of the Complete Psychological Works of Sigmund Freud,* vol. XIV (1914–1916), trans. James Strachey (London: Hogarth Press and the Institute for

Psychoanalysis, 1957), 243, www.english.upenn.edu/
~cavitch/pdf-library/Freud_MourningAndMelancholia.pdf.

3. Ibid., 245.

4. Sigmund Freud, quoted in Phyllis R. Silverman and
Dennis Klass, "Introduction: What's the Problem?" in
Continuing Bonds: New Understandings of Grief, eds.
Dennis Klass, Phyllis R. Silverman, and Steven L.
Nickman (New York: Taylor & Francis Group, 1996), 6.

5. Erich Lindemann, "Symptomatology and Management
of Acute Grief," *American Journal of Psychiatry 101* (1944),
141–148, nyu.edu/classes/gmoran/LINDEMANN.pdf.

6. Elisabeth Kübler-Ross, *On Death and Dying: What the
Dying Have to Teach Doctors, Nurses, Clergy, and Their
Own Families* (New York: Scribner, 1969), 11.

7. Ibid., 52.

8. Ibid., 63.

9. Ibid., 93.

10. Ibid., 97.

11. Ibid., 123–24.

12. "Stage Theory," *Encyclopedia of Death and Dying,*
deathreference.com/Sh-Sy/Stage-Theory.html.

13. Quoted in Ruth Davis Konigsberg, *The Truth About
Grief: The Myth of Its Five Stages and the New Science of
Loss* (New York: Simon & Schuster Paperback, 2011), 9.

14. Ibid., 3.

15. Ibid., 2.

16. Emily Eaton, "The Myth of the 'Five Stages of
Grief,'" *Creating "NewNormal"* (blog), December
1, 2011, creatingnewnormal.com/2011/12/01/
the-myth-of-the-five-stages-of-grief/.

17. Megan Devine, "The 5 Stages of Grief and Other
Lies That Don't Help Anyone," *The Huffington Post,*

December 11, 2013, huffingtonpost.com/megan-devine/
stages-of-grief_b_4414077.html.

18. William Worden, *Grief Counseling and Grief Therapy*
(New York: Springer, 1982).

Chapter 3: The Way Forward Through Stories

1. Dennis Klass, Phyllis R. Silverman, and Steven Nickman,
eds., *Continuing Bonds: New Understandings of Grief*
(New York: Taylor & Francis Group, 1996).

2. Ibid., xviii.

3. Ibid., 17.

Chapter 4: On the Right Path

1. Joan Didion, *The Year of Magical Thinking* (New York:
Alfred A. Knopf, 2005), 6–7.

2. Ibid., 9–10.

3. Ibid., 225.

4. Meghan O'Rourke. *The Long Goodbye: A Memoir* (New
York: Riverhead Books, 2011), 119.

5. Ibid., 217.

6. Scott Simon, *Unforgettable: A Son, A Mother, and the
Lessons of a Lifetime* (New York: Flatiron Books, 2015),
234–35.

7. Edward Hirsch, *Gabriel: A Poem* (New York: Alfred A
Knopf, 2014), 73.

8. Candi K. Cann, *Virtual Afterlives: Grieving the Dead
in the Twenty-First Century* (Lexington: The University
Press of Kentucky, 2014).

9. Candi K. Cann, "Responding Theologically to
Contemporary Mourning," *Cosmologics,* Spring 2015,
cosmologicsmagazine.com/candi-k-cann-responding-
theologically-to-contemporary-mourning/.

10. Candi K. Cann, interview with Tim Madigan, August 16, 2016.

11. Ibid.

12. Rita Charon, *Narrative Medicine: Honoring the Stories of Illness* (New York: Oxford University Press, 2006).

13. "Honoring the Stories of Illness | Dr. Rita Charon | TEDxAtlanta," YouTube video, 18:16, presentation at TEDxAtlanta, posted by "TEDx Talks," November 4, 2011, www.youtube.com/watch?v=24kHX2HtU3o.

14. Ibid.

15. Rita Charon, interview with Tim Madigan, September 7, 2016.

Chapter 6: Know Thyself

1. *Funk & Wagnalls New Comprehensive International Dictionary of the English Language,* Deluxe ed., s.v. "grief."

2. Alan Wolfelt, *Counseling Skills for Companioning the Mourner* (Fort Collins, CO: Companion Press, 2016), 7.

3. *Macbeth,* in *William Shakespeare: The Complete Works,* ed. Alfred Harbage (Baltimore, MD: Penguin Books, 1969), 4.3.1130. References are to act, scene, and page.

Chapter 8: Attachment and Grief

1. Tim Lawrence, "The Pain of Feeling Inadequate," *The Adversity Within* (blog), February 10, 2016, timjlawrence.com/blog/2016/2/8/inadequate. The quote "Grief really is love, weeping" appears in Lawrence's response to a reader comment on his original post.

2. John Bowlby, *Loss: Sadness and Depression* (New York: Basic Books, 1980).

3. Louis Cozolino, *The Neuroscience of Psychotherapy: Healing the Social Brain,* 2nd ed. (New York: W.W. Norton, 2010), 224.

4. John Prendergast, *In Touch: How to Tune In to the Inner Guidance of Your Body and Trust Yourself* (Boulder, CO: Sounds True, 2015), 5.

5. Ibid., 6.

6. Kenneth Doka, ed. *Disenfranchised Grief: New Directions, Challenges, and Strategies for Practice* (Champaign, IL: Research Press, 2002), xiii.

Chapter 9: Your Story

1. Tim Madigan, *I'm Proud of You: My Friendship with Fred Rogers* (Los Angeles: Ubuntu Press, 2012), 131–32.

2. Ibid., 132–33.

Chapter 10: The Culture of Positivity

1. Meghan O'Rourke and Leeat Granek, "How to Help Friends in Mourning," *Slate,* August 4, 2011, slate.com/articles/life/grieving/2011/08/how_to_help_friends_in_mourning.html.

2. Fred Rogers, "Thoughts for All Ages," *PBS Kids* (online article), pbskids.org/rogers/nonflash/all_ages/thoughts4.htm.

3. C. S. Lewis, *A Grief Observed* (London: Farber, 1961), 12–13.

4. Stephen L. Salter, "The Culture of Positivity and the Mistreatment of Trauma," *NetworkTherapy. com: A Mental Health Network*, April 17, 2013, networktherapy.com/library/articles/Culture-of-Positivity-and-the-Mistreatment-of-Trauma/.

5. Barbara Ehrenreich, *Bright-Sided: How the Relentless Promotion of Positive Thinking Has Undermined America* (New York: Metropolitan Books, 2009), 12–13.

6. Ibid., 89.

7. Joel Osteen, *Your Best Life Now: 7 Steps to Living at Your Full Potential* (New York: Warner Books, 2004), 263–64.

8. Joanne Cacciatore, "Be Like the Little Children: An Open Letter to Pastor Joel Osteen," *Becoming* (blog), June 2013, drjoanne.blogspot.com/2015/06/be-like-little-children-open-letter-to.html.

9. Francis Weller, *The Wild Edge of Sorrow* (Berkeley, CA: North Atlantic Books, 2015), xix.

10. Thomas Long and Thomas Lynch, *The Good Funeral: Death, Grief, and the Community of Care* (Louisville, KY: Westminster John Knox Press, 2013), 59–60.

11. Ibid., 96.

12. Fred Rogers, *The World According to Mister Rogers: Important Things to Remember* (New York: Hachette Books), 20.

13. O'Rourke and Granek, "How to Help Friends in Mourning."

Chapter 11: The Expectations of Others

1. While I have had experiences with grieving clients of most of the major religious groups, I feel most qualified to speak to the experience of those who are members of Christian churches. Therefore, I cannot offer examples of what grief support looks like in other faith communities.

Chapter 12: Help for the Helper

1. Donald McNeill, Douglas Morrison, and Henri Nouwen, *Compassion: A Reflection on the Christian Life* (New York: Doubleday, 1983), 3–4.

2. Alan D. Wolfelt, *Companioning the Bereaved: A Soulful Guide for Caregivers* (Fort Collins, CO: Companion Press, 2006), 27.

3. Louis Cozolino, *The Neuroscience of Psychotherapy: Healing the Social Brain,* 2nd ed. (New York: W.W. Norton, 2010), 25.
4. Daniel Goleman, *Social Intelligence: The New Science of Human Relationships* (New York: Bantam Dell, 2006), 88.
5. John Prendergast, *In Touch: How to Tune In to the Inner Guidance of Your Body and Trust Yourself* (Boulder, CO: Sounds True, 2015), 4.

Chapter 13: Sorrows Shared

1. Tim Madigan, *I'm Proud of You: My Friendship with Fred Rogers* (Los Angeles: Ubuntu Press, 2012), 59–61.
2. Henri Nouwen, "What Is Most Personal Is Most Universal," Henri Nouwen Society website, February 23, 2016, henrinouwen.org/meditation/what-is-most-personal-is-most-universal/.
3. *As You Like It,* in *William Shakespeare: The Complete Works,* ed. Alfred Harbage (Baltimore, MD: Penguin Books, 1969), 2.7.257. References are to act, scene, and page.
4. Michael Gingerich and Thomas Kaden, *Someone to Tell It To: Sharing Life's Journey* (Nashville: WestBow Press, 2014), xi.
5. Ibid.

Chapter 14: A Therapist Grieves Still

1. Ronald Knapp, *Beyond Endurance,* 2nd ed. (Bloomington, IN: Author House, 2005), 43.

Epilogue

1. Patrick O'Malley, "Getting Grief Right," *New York Times,* January 10, 2015, opinionator.blogs.nytimes.com/2015/01/10/getting-grief-right/?_r=0.

FURTHER READING

My favorite books about loss, written by writers and journalists:

Deraniyagala, Sonali. *Wave*. New York: Alfred A Knopf, 2013.

Didion, Joan. *The Year of Magical Thinking*. New York: Random House, 2005.

Hirsch, Edward. *Gabriel: A Poem*. New York: Alfred A. Knopf, 2014.

Lewis, C. S. *A Grief Observed*. London: Faber and Faber, 1961.

Madigan, Tim. *I'm Proud of You: My Friendship with Fred Rogers*. Los Angeles: Ubuntu Press, 2012.

O'Rourke, Meghan. *The Long Goodbye: A Memoir*. New York: Riverhead Books, 2011.

Rehm, Diane. *On My Own*. New York: Alfred A Knopf, 2016.

Rosenblatt, Roger. *Kayak Morning*. New York: Harper Collins, 2011.

Rosenblatt, Roger. *Making Toast*. New York: Harper Collins, 2010.

Simon, Scott. *Unforgettable: A Son, A Mother, and the Lessons of a Lifetime*. New York: Flatiron Books, 2015.

Starr, Mirabai. *Caravan of No Despair*. Boulder, CO: Sounds True, 2015.

Strayed, Cheryl. *Wild*. New York: Vintage Books, 2013.

Appendix I

SEEKING HELP

A referral from a trusted person is the best way to find the right mental health professional. Seek the advice of clergy, a physician, or a friend who is familiar with therapy. If you are in a grief support group, ask other members for referral suggestions. I recommend interviewing prospective counselors over the telephone before your first visit. With the knowledge gained from this book, ask about their approach to working with grieving clients and whether they subscribe to theories like the stages of grief or promote ideas such as closure or acceptance. If so, they might not be the person for you. Ask about their experience helping trauma victims. Try to determine whether the counselor is a person of compassion and empathy and a good listener. That might be their greatest credential of all.

Support groups come in two varieties—continuous and time limited. Many faith communities offer time-limited groups, often during the holiday season. Continuous groups usually have a primary theme, like the death of a child or spouse. The Compassionate Friends, for example, is an umbrella organization for a worldwide network of support groups for those grieving the death of a child. Most large cities have a support group clearinghouse through their United Way affiliate.

THE VOCABULARY OF GRIEF

What follows are words adapted from The WARM Place training manual and words I've heard my grieving clients use repeatedly over the years when discussing their experience. These might be helpful as a reminder that although loss affects our body, emotions, and mind, all of that is to be expected.

Physical or Behavioral

- Being accident prone
- Cold hands
- Compromised immune system
- Dry mouth
- Gastrointestinal discomfort
- Headaches
- Insomnia
- Loss of appetite
- Low energy
- Muscle tightness
- Muscle weakness
- Nightmares
- Numb or tingling extremities
- Overeating
- Oversleeping
- Rapid heartbeat
- Shortness of breath
- Sighing
- Slowed speech
- Sweating
- Sweaty palms
- Tearfulness
- Trembling
- Undereating
- Undersleeping

Emotional or Social

- Agitation
- Anger
- Anxiousness—general or specific
- Blaming others
- Crying
- Dread of social engagements
- Feelings of worthlessness
- Guilt
- Indecisiveness
- Irritability
- Isolation from friends and family
- Lack of initiative
- Low self-esteem
- Moodiness
- Relationship stress
- Restlessness
- Shame
- Unexpected outbursts

Cognitive

- Confusion
- Daydreaming
- Errors in judgment
- Errors in language
- Forgetfulness
- Inattention
- Loss of creativity
- Memory loss
- Mental blocking
- Overachievement
- Preoccupation
- Rumination

Getting Grief Right

STUDY GUIDE
For Groups and Individuals

INTRODUCTION

The purpose of this study guide is to help you build on the experience of *Getting Grief Right* and to connect even more deeply with your story of loss. But don't misinterpret the suggested exercises that follow. It can't be said enough that loss is not an experience to "work through"; rather, it is a story about a relationship that has changed through death. That story, in turn, becomes part of the larger story of the rest of your life.

It is my wish that you find additional meaning and insight here, but not in the sense of finding the study guide prescriptive or in the hope that it will help you reach resolution or acceptance. And, of course, there is no right or wrong answer to the study guide questions.

From my long experience working with grieving people, I'm confident that the guide will (1) cause you to think about aspects of your story that you haven't previously; (2) help you retrieve memories about your story that will be helpful in understanding your relationship to the one you lost and, therefore, the nature of your grief; (3) inspire new questions that stimulate further reflection on your loss narrative; (4) help you organize your story from its many parts into a more cohesive whole; and (5) help you further appreciate that your grief story continues, and it always will in some way.

The study guide can be used in any number of ways—by individuals, by existing support groups, or by new groups formed by readers of this book.

If your preference is to move through the study guide on your own or if you don't have access to others who might join you, I hope you will eventually have the opportunity to share your story of loss with a trusted other. It is one thing for you to fully understand, embrace, and affirm your own experience. But we all crave to have the inner parts of our being—especially the painful ones—acknowledged and affirmed by others. In addition, others can help us interpret our stories in ways that we might not be able to ourselves.

That act of trust and sharing is a great reward in itself. Few human interactions are as nourishing or profound as that kind of intimacy. It is something I am grateful to experience every day with my clients. That's not to say that sharing your grief story with another will be easy. Just as it's not easy for my clients to step through the doors of my office for the first time, it will take courage for you to reach out. But don't deprive yourself of the experience. In the pages to come, I give you further guidance for how your story can be told and received.

Existing support groups are invited to use *Getting Grief Right* and its study guide according to their own needs and practices, focusing on whatever information might be useful or relevant. But this guide is most tailored for those who choose to form their own *Getting Grief Right* support or discussion group. In the pages to come, I set out quite specific suggestions about how your group should be structured and operate. Again, nothing is set in stone, but I strongly encourage you to try to follow the roadmap laid out here. Basic structure and rules are essential for creating a safe, supportive environment for grieving people who come together to share their hearts.

Getting Grief Right and this study guide draw upon and reinforce our instinctual desire to give meaning to our lives through story. In the following pages, let that story be gently drawn out of you. Some questions and exercises will be more relevant to you than others. Some may affect you in ways you did not expect. Let them. There is no pressure to accomplish a goal or complete a task. And you are the only expert on you.

HOW TO USE THIS GUIDE

Individuals

If you have read the book, you probably have begun the process of finding and connecting with the story of your loss. The recommended journaling might have been particularly helpful in this regard. In the pages that follow, I suggest a series of six meetings for *Getting Grief Right* support groups, with suggested topics and agendas for each meeting. As an individual, you are invited to approach the material in the same way, meeting by meeting, making use of the same review materials and questions to deepen and organize the exploration of your story.

Again, I strongly encourage you to put your thoughts and feelings in writing. Although you might not be subject to a group schedule, it's important to devote specific time to read, think about, and respond to the questions in the study guide. You honor yourself and the one you lost by carving time out of your day or week. Find a calm, peaceful environment where you can reflect on and express the emotions of your loss.

After you finish with the study guide, you can reach out to share your story of loss in any number of ways. Reflect on the people who have best supported you in your grief so far, who have been safe and attentive. Perhaps it was a friend, sibling, clergy member, or coworker who seemed to know intuitively how to listen and who knew what you needed. Tell that person that you have found this book helpful and ask if they will read it, particularly chapter 12, "Help for the Helper." Then ask whether they would be willing to receive your narrative, either by reading what you've written or by listening as you read it to them.

Tell them that all you require is for them to listen attentively. Gentle affirmation of your story would be wonderful, but the listening is most important. Encourage questions that arise naturally, but tell listeners that they should avoid judgment of any kind and should not give advice unless you request it. Odds are, the person you have chosen will likely know exactly what to do. Your story can be shared over a series of meetings at a coffee shop, on a park bench, or in the living room of your home—whatever is most comfortable for you.

Established Support Groups

This study guide can also be a valuable resource for members of existing support groups. It is not necessary that group members read the book. Study guide questions, standing alone, will be helpful to those attempting to explore the experience of grief. I foresee groups like The Compassionate Friends or Survivors of Suicide using the study guide to facilitate small-group discussion. The same can be true for existing grief groups in churches, synagogues, and mosques.

If existing support groups choose to engage with the study guide more systematically, from beginning to end, I strongly recommend that members adopt my suggestions for how to proceed and adhere to the suggested meeting schedule.

COMING TOGETHER

Why Come Together?

Before we discuss the formation of *Getting Grief Right* support groups, it might be helpful to reflect on why such gatherings are helpful.

Support groups offer care and support for those who share a common burden. The comfort is based on the assumption that those who share similar experiences will be able to understand and empathize in ways that others cannot. Support groups have proliferated in the past few decades because of the isolation so many feel in the modern world, combined with the deep human need for connection.

A simple Internet search provides a menu of groups for those who suffer from addiction, mood disorders, medical illnesses, behavioral problems, and, of course, bereavement. Grief support groups exist to fill a void for those who feel isolated in their mourning. It is typical in our culture for a person's friends and family to prematurely withdraw support from a grieving person. Many others who mourn lack any kind of support from their community. Thus, a support group can be an essential surrogate.

Getting Started

Groups can be organized around specific types of loss (suicide, murder, accident, illness), or they could be open to those who have suffered losses of any kind. I believe this study guide will be helpful to either type of group. Survivors of suicide, for example, will have a common frame of reference that could promote deeper understanding, particularly when it comes to issues like guilt; there are obvious benefits to that. An open group underscores the reality of the universality of loss and the many forms it can take. Whatever your preference, the stories of grief will connect at some level and diverge at many others. What's most important is that members commit to sharing and listening with an open mind and heart.

My experience suggests that people should wait at least six months before joining a support group. The newly bereaved are more likely to find the experience overwhelming, and it will be more difficult for them to speak of their loss. They also will be less likely to have the energy to receive the stories of others, which is necessary for participation.

Limiting group size is also essential. I strongly recommend that groups consist of no more than five members, so that each person has sufficient time to share in the meetings.

Meetings should be limited to ninety minutes and should end on time. Longer meetings, especially when members are discussing matters that are so private and potentially emotional, raise the risk of "sharing fatigue."

To find members, start by sharing *Getting Grief Right* with friends who also have experienced loss. Then suggest coming together to explore the lessons of the book more deeply. If you belong to a faith community, consider asking a clergy member or other religious leader to read the book; then, invite grieving congregation members to come together. Potential members could be found in other support or recovery groups. Facebook and other social media sites are other tools to find members.

The meeting place should be peaceful and private. Soft lighting and comfortable chairs are ideal. Meeting in a circle or around a table, where all members can easily make eye contact, creates an environment of safety and openness. Sharing a meal before the meeting or coffee or snacks afterward can further enhance the sense of community.

Where practical, a mental health professional could be asked to lead and moderate the storytelling meetings. But any group member can take on that role, or the role of leader/moderator can be rotated among members.

This guide provides outlines for the structure of six meetings, which could be held weekly or, if necessary, every other week. Each meeting is designed to be ninety minutes, which should allow enough time for each of the two to five members to express themselves. Again, the time frame and structure are essential. Without these parameters, it is easy for group members to get off track or become overwhelmed, which, in turn, affects your ability to provide true support for one another.

Group Agreements

Emotional safety is imperative to any support group. Each person must feel confident that they will not be judged or criticized and that what they share will remain in confidence with other group members.

Relationships among group members will evolve. Depending on the familiarity of the group members before they come together, there may be periods of discomfort and awkwardness as they get to know one another. This is perfectly normal and necessary as the members develop a culture of trust. I'm confident that rapport will develop quickly; to that end, however, it's important to adhere to the rules and structure.

Group members should reread chapter 12 of *Getting Grief Right*, preferably before the first meeting and no later than the second.

That common frame of reference will be very important. Group members should also agree to the following:

1. Be prompt and commit to attend all meetings.

2. Be respectful of time constraints, and do not take more than the allotted minutes to share.

3. Acknowledge that all members' loss narratives are unique and are to be respected as such. The thoughts and feelings shared by group members are neither right nor wrong.

4. Be willing to sit quietly in the presence of another's emotion or pain and to quietly offer appropriate comfort and support.

5. Respect any group member's request not to share.

6. Be open to share your own story to the degree you are comfortable. Be willing to stretch toward deeper disclosure as the group evolves.

7. Listen with an open heart to the stories of others. Ask questions primarily for clarification and to deepen understanding of another's experience. Do not give advice unless the group member specifically requests it.

8. Honor privacy and confidentiality. This is crucial for creating emotional safety. Nothing discussed in the meeting should ever leave the meeting room.

MEETING 1

The leader starts the meeting at the appointed time by asking for a few moments of silence; this marks a time of transition from the bustle of the everyday world.

The leader then introduces him- or herself and invites the others to do the same. Introductions should include the following information:

- First name only

- Relationship to the person who died

- The date and circumstances of a loved one's death

When all members have been introduced, the leader reads the group agreements and asks each member to commit to them.

In about five minutes, the leader briefly answers the following questions and then invites the others to do the same.

- Why were you drawn to the group?

- Do you have any concerns?

- What are your expectations?

After each member has spoken, the leader reminds the group of the meeting schedule. If leadership is to be rotated, assignments for future meetings can be made.

The leader then introduces a discussion on how the group will operate, preferably based on my suggestions:

> *The purpose of the group is to allow each member to orally share the three chapters of their story of grief within the structure of the meetings. Every week there will be an agenda, so that you all can discuss similar parts of your grief stories—that is, your attachment or the circumstances of death. Every week will include review material and questions to deepen your exploration of your own story.*

At each meeting, I recommend that sharing occur in rounds. The length of time a person has to share is dictated by the size of the group. For instance, in a group of four, each member will have roughly ten minutes per round to speak, including time for a few follow-up questions or words of affirmation from the others.

Every week, members will be asked to review chapters in the book, to read client stories, and to consider a list of questions from the study guide. Members should focus only on those stories or questions relevant to their own experience and should write about the feelings and memories inspired by the material.

Given the time constraints, I suggest that members share what they consider to be the most important aspects of their grief story first. It is the leader's responsibility to remind members when they have come close to using their allotted time. Flexibility should be allowed if a member becomes emotional or clearly needs additional time or support. However, every effort should be made to ensure that all members have an equal chance to speak and that the meeting concludes on time. An agreed-upon hand signal by the facilitator can alert the one speaking that a minute or so is left for sharing.

All members should understand that if a person does not get to share something that they feel is important, they should note that to the group before the meeting adjourns. Then the facilitator will make sure time is allotted for them to share early in the next meeting.

The leader then lays out the agenda for the next week, which includes sharing the story of attachment, reflections on how an individual's personality affects their way of grieving, and what, if any, previous experience each member had with death.

Preparation for Meeting 2

For the next meeting, members are encouraged to bring photos or items emblematic of their attachment to the one who died. Suggested reading for Meeting 2 includes chapter 6, "Know Thyself" and chapter 8, "Attachment and Grief." Also review the stories of Mary (introduction and chapter 3), Scott (chapter 3), Margaret (chapter 8), John and Liz (chapter 6), Carol (chapter 7), Martha (chapter 11), and of my grandmother's suicide (chapter 7).

Members should review and reflect on questions listed under Meeting 2 and write out their stories. They can use what they have read as a reference when they are speaking, or they can read their stories verbatim to the group, according to their preference.

Close

The leader concludes the first meeting by reminding members of the need for confidentiality. Other housekeeping matters, such as organizing refreshments for the next meeting or plans for social time before and after a meeting, are discussed last.

Each meeting ends with a few seconds of silence to help transition back to the daily world. Mutual congratulations should be offered, as coming to a group of fellow mourners requires courage.

MEETING 2

After an opening period of silence, the leader shares the following focus and structure for the meeting.

The focus of Meeting 2 is to share the first chapter of your loss story, as described in Getting Grief Right. *Your first chapter is about attachment to the one who died. The bereaved person's life with you may have lasted only hours, or it may have stretched out over many decades. It may have been pure, wonderful, deeply loving, or it could have been very complicated and riddled with conflict. Again, all members must set judgment aside and listen with an open mind and heart.*

In this session, members are invited to discuss their understanding of how basic personality types and family culture have played into their grief experiences.

Storytelling: Round 1

In the allotted time, each group member shares his or her story of attachment to the one who died. Each member is also invited to share a photograph of the person who died or a keepsake emblematic of the member's attachment. I suggest that in describing that attachment, members start at the beginning of the relationship—be it the birth of a child, the first memory, or the day of meeting. Members are invited to focus on how their attachment was unique, the aspects of it for which they are grateful, and their conflicts with the one they lost. The following questions may help shape this chapter of the narrative. Members should focus on the questions that are most relevant to their own experience.

- What did this relationship mean to you? How was the attachment special and unique?

- How did you connect emotionally, spiritually, intellectually, recreationally? What other ways did you connect?

- Who could you be with that person that you could not be with any other?

- How did you spend time together?

- How would you describe the personality of the one who died?

- What is your favorite story about him?

- What was it about her that made you feel safe or valued?

- What was his greatest joy or sorrow?

- What important values did you share? Where did your values diverge?

- If there was conflict, how was it managed?

- Was your attachment close and deep, like Scott's with his father (see chapter 3)?

- Was there conflict or ill will, such as between Margaret and her mother (see chapter 8) or Carol and her sister (see chapter 7)?

Storytelling: Round 2

In the second round, members are asked to tell the story of their own personality and how it has affected their experience and expression of grief. The following questions might be helpful.

- Do you consider yourself:
  › Extroverted or introverted?
  › Emotional or cerebral?
  › A risk taker or cautious?
  › High energy or low energy?
  › Conservative or liberal?
  › Methodical or spontaneous?
  › Prone to anxiety or depression?

- Do you see any similarity between yourself and Mary (see introduction and chapter 3), who put pressure on herself to get her grief right?

- Would you describe yourself more like John or Liz (see chapter 6)?

- Describe the similarities and differences of other friends or family members who grieve the same loss.

Storytelling: Round 3

In the third round of discussion, members should share their grief story as it concerns their previous experience with death and the culture of their family of origin.

- What is your first memory about death?

- Had you suffered other significant losses before the one you currently grieve?

- How would you describe the culture of your family of origin as it relates to death and grieving?

- Is your family open about expressing loss or mourning, or averse to it?

- Does your family have rituals associated with death and bereavement? If so, what are they?

- In Martha's family (see chapter 11), grief was seen as "negative." Where does your family fall on the scale of positivity?

- Does your family have death secrets from previous generations that have created an untold story, similar to the one that haunted the author's father (see chapter 7)?

Preparation for Meeting 3

At the end of the third round of discussion, the leader introduces the agenda and topics for the next meeting, which will focus on the circumstances of death and its immediate aftermath. Members are asked to review the Meeting 3 questions and chapters 7 and 8. They should also review the stories of Tim (chapter 9); Kara, Jack and Tara, and Steven and Marissa (chapter 7); and "Lars" and Casey and his friend Bob (chapter 12).

The leader closes the meeting with a few seconds of silence.

MEETING 3

After an opening period of silence, the leader can share the following focus and structure for the meeting.

The focus of this meeting is the second chapter of the story of loss, the circumstances of death, and the immediate aftermath.

Storytelling: Round 1
In this first round, members describe the circumstances of the death of their loved one.

- Was the death sudden or anticipated?

- How did you learn of the death?

- If you were present, what do you remember hearing, smelling, and seeing in the moments surrounding the death?

- Was it a peaceful death with little to no trauma, or did you experience some level of trauma? Describe it. Could you relate to anything in the stories of Tim, Kara, Jack and Tara, or Steven and Marissa?

- Did the death challenge your faith? If so, how?

Storytelling: Round 2

In the second round, members describe what they remember most about the days and weeks after the death.

- Did people gather at your home?

- Was there a visitation or wake?

- Was there a service? What type of service? How did you feel about it?

- How long did you take off from work or other activities? Did it feel like a helpful and necessary amount of time? If not, how long do you wish you had had before returning to work or activities?

- What were the most challenging aspects of your return to daily life?

Storytelling: Round 3

- Who was there for you during the death event and the weeks that followed?

- Who surprised you with their presence or their absence in the early days of loss?

- How did others, such as acquaintances or coworkers, respond to you in the days and weeks after the death?

- Could you relate to the experience of "Lars" and Casey (see chapter 12)?

- Whose support were you particularly grateful for?

Preparation for Meeting 4

At the conclusion of Meeting 3, the leader assigns support material for the following week's storytelling, which will focus on the third chapter of the grief narrative. The material includes reading the discussion questions set forth for Meeting 4; review of chapter 9, which describes the third chapter of the grief story; and review of chapter 5 on environmental triggers. Members should also review the stories of Suzanne (chapter 2), Brenda (chapter 5), Mark and Anne (chapter 8), and Linda (chapter 11), as well as appendix II, "The Vocabulary of Grief."

The leader closes the meeting with a few seconds of silence.

MEETING 4

After an opening period of silence, the leader can share the following focus and structure for the meeting.

Chapter 3 of your grief narrative will be the focus of this meeting and the next. In this meeting, you will be asked to share your individual experience of loss. The communal experience of loss will be explored next week.

Storytelling: Round 1

As a review of the Vocabulary of Grief, members discuss the following questions (see appendix II):

- What did you notice about yourself in the three categories: physical/behavioral, emotional/social, and cognitive? Are there words that describe your grief that aren't listed in the appendix?

- How has your personality affected the expression of your grief?

- What sights, sounds, scents, and touch suddenly remind you of the one you lost? What are the most common reminders, sights, sounds, and scents that you come across multiple times a day?

- What aspects of your environment cause you to feel particularly connected to him or her? Have you felt overwhelmed by environmental triggers, like Brenda did (see chapter 5)?

- Did you have to manage the possessions of the one who died? If so, what was that like? What items did you decide to keep?

- How have you experienced the "firsts" (birthdays, anniversaries, or holidays)?

- Did you play a specific role with the one who died, such as caregiver, grandparent, or work partner? Is that a role you now miss?

- Has your loss changed how you attach in new relationships?

Storytelling: Round 2

Mourning is the expression of grief. In this round, members discuss how they have expressed their grief.

- Did you self-analyze your grief like Suzanne (see chapter 2)? If so, what concerned you about your grief response? What confused you? What surprised you? Have you felt any embarrassment or shame about your grief?

- Have you experienced any guilt or regret? If so, describe it.

- Describe your experience of social splitting, when you needed to act better than you felt, like Linda (see chapter 11).

- Some who mourn resist the idea of "staying busy." Some find staying busy helpful. How do you feel?

- What are the healthy and unhealthy ways you have responded to stress in the past? Have you engaged in any of those behaviors during your time of grief?

- Have you found ways to be compassionate to yourself? If so, how?

- Have there been added stressors as a result of your loss, such as a change in finances or a need to relocate? If so, what are they?

- Did you experience "disenfranchised grief," like Mark or Anne (see chapter 8)?

- How has your loss changed you? Have your values, priorities, faith, or relationships shifted? If so, how?

- Has your loss changed how you respond to others who have experienced loss? If so how?

Preparation for Meeting 5

Members are encouraged to read the discussion questions for Meeting 5. They should also review chapters 9 and 11 and the stories of Vickie, Joanne, Brad, and Tad and Maria (chapter 11).

The leader closes the meeting with a few seconds of silence.

MEETING 5

After an opening period of silence, the leader can share the following focus and structure for the meeting.

The focus now is the grief story as it relates to your own experience in community.

Storytelling

* Looking back, what have been your unmet needs since your loss?

* Have you noticed that your level of support has changed or diminished over time? If so, how? How does that make you feel?

* Describe how your immediate family has mourned together or separately. How has that affected you?

* Who has best supported you in the time since your loss?

* How often do you hear the name of the one you lost? Is it enough?

- What was the most helpful, comforting thing you've been told by another since your loss?

- Have you been supported on social media? Has that been a genuine comfort?

- Have you heard clichés of loss from others? If so, how did they make you feel?

- Has someone asked you about your loved one, not knowing that they had died? If so, how did you feel? What did you say?

- How were you supported, or not supported, by your faith community? Could you relate to the experience of Vickie or Joanne (see chapter 11)? How did you respond to or manage painful people or experiences in your religious community?

- Did you find any comments shocking, offensive, or particularly troubling? If so, how did you respond?

- Did you have any tension with friends or family because of how they responded to your loss? What was it like?

- Did you experience any "loss within the loss," such as estrangement from a family member or friend, like Brad (see chapter 11)? How did the estrangement occur?

- Was anyone in your community a self-centered helper or energy drain, like the friend of Tad and

Maria (see chapter 11)? How did you manage that person or those people?

- Now that you have been through it yourself, what do you wish the community as a whole understood about grief and mourning?

Preparation for Meeting 6

In the last meeting, members can summarize their stories or discuss anything about their loss that might not have come up earlier. To that end, the questions for Meeting 6 might be helpful. Tell members that at the last meeting, they will be encouraged to share any grief books, poems, songs, movies, support groups, or websites that have been meaningful in their grief journey.

The leader closes the meeting with a few seconds of silence.

MEETING 6

After an opening period of silence, the leader can share the following focus and structure for the meeting.

The focus of this meeting is to review, summarize, and say goodbye. Before discussion begins, any group member who has not had a chance to share storytelling from previous meetings will have the opportunity to do so.

Storytelling: Round 1

- What, if anything, has surprised you about your grief story?

- How have your grief and mourning changed in the time since your loss? What do you wish would change? What do you hope will not change?

- Do you currently have one or more persons in your life with whom you can continue to share your loss story? If not, where might you find such a person?

- What books, poems, songs, movies, websites, or support groups have been meaningful to you in your grief? Why?

- Has your loss inspired you to do volunteer work? If so, what has that been, and how has the experience been meaningful?

Storytelling: Round 2

- How would you describe your overall experience with this group?

- Was there anything you needed that you did not receive?

- Were any specific aspects of the group, or parts of your story, particularly challenging or difficult to share?

- What did you find most helpful? Why?

- Did you find any specific discussions helpful?

Moving Forward

In a concluding discussion, members can decide if they wish to continue to meet and, if so, on what schedule. Some may feel like the six-week experience has been sufficient and may not need future contact. Their decision should be supported.

Close

In one last round of sharing, members are encouraged to say their goodbyes to one another. Any final appreciation or gratitude for the other group members or the experience of participating in this sacred group of mourners may be shared.

End the meeting with a closing silence.

ACKNOWLEDGMENTS

When I pitched the idea of this book to my long-time friend Tim Madigan about ten years ago, he immediately volunteered to help me tell the story of a new way of viewing grief. The demands of two busy lives were such that it was not until a couple of years ago that our collaboration really began. I'm deeply indebted to Tim for his belief in me and in this book. His skill as an interviewer transformed my story from the clinical to the personal and from the abstract to the practical. In the process, our friendship has deepened, for which I am also very grateful.

My literary agent, Linda Konner, also believed in this story from the beginning. Her knowledge, skill, and persistence helped me find the perfect publishing home. My editor at Sounds True, Amy Rost, brought an exceptional level of insight, intuition, and wisdom to this project. *Getting Grief Right* was truly a collaboration with her and the talented Sounds True team.

Dr. Rita Charon and Dr. Candi Cann generously shared their time and insights in long conversations. Their work inspires me, and their belief in the purpose and power of story mirrors my own.

My deepest thanks to Peggy Bohme, cofounder of The WARM Place, who invited me, in 1989, to contribute to a wonderful mission, working with grieving children and their families. For nineteen years, as I taught WARM Place volunteers, my ideas about grieving evolved and were greatly clarified.

I am, of course, grateful for the love of my family and friends. Their enthusiasm and curiosity have sustained me through the writing of this book.

I am indebted to the many physicians, clergy, educators, and colleagues who have referred grieving clients to me over the decades. These bereaved individuals, couples, and families have opened their hearts and shared their most vulnerable selves with me. I have been privileged to be a part of their sacred pilgrimage of loss.

My wife, Nancy, has been my companion in this and every other story of my adult life. It is an act of love and generosity that she entrusted me to share our most painful personal loss with readers she will never know. She did so with the desire and belief that this book could be helpful for those who grieve. She lovingly had identical rings made for us to commemorate the first anniversary of our son's death. Our rings have three interweaving gold bands representing the eternal bond of our relationship to him and his to us. This beautiful expression of her love for him and her love for me reminds me daily of how fortunate I am that I get to be her husband.

ABOUT THE AUTHORS

Patrick O'Malley has been providing grief counseling and education to clients, volunteers, and colleagues for more than thirty-five years. He has also served as a consultant to physician practices, attorneys, and businesses and has several professional publications on grief and professional ethics. He lives in Fort Worth, Texas, with his wife, Nancy. For more information, visit drpatrickomalley.com.

Tim Madigan is an award-winning Texas newspaper journalist and author of four books, including *The Burning: Massacre, Destruction, and the Tulsa Race Riot of 1921; I'm Proud of You: My Friendship with Fred Rogers;* and *Every Common Sight: a Novel.* He lives in Fort Worth, Texas, with his wife, Catherine. For more, visit timmadigan.net.

ABOUT SOUNDS TRUE

Sounds True is a multimedia publisher whose mission is to inspire and support personal transformation and spiritual awakening. Founded in 1985 and located in Boulder, Colorado, we work with many of the leading spiritual teachers, thinkers, healers, and visionary artists of our time. We strive with every title to preserve the essential "living wisdom" of the author or artist. It is our goal to create products that not only provide information to a reader or listener, but that also embody the quality of a wisdom transmission.

For those seeking genuine transformation, Sounds True is your trusted partner. At SoundsTrue.com you will find a wealth of free resources to support your journey, including exclusive weekly audio interviews, free downloads, interactive learning tools, and other special savings on all our titles.

To learn more, please visit SoundsTrue.com/freegifts or call us toll-free at 800.333.9185.

SOUNDS TRUE
many voices, one journey